FIRE AN

A Journey of Survival and Resilience

By

Imee R. Warren

Copyright © 2024 by Imee R. Warren

All rights reserved. This book or any portion thereof may not be reproduced or used in any manner whatsoever without the publisher's express written permission except for using brief quotations in a book review.

This book is dedicated to all the people who supported me throughout my adversities.

I especially want to thank my husband, James, for being by my side, for tirelessly supporting me during my weeks in the hospital, as well as the continuing journey to recovery and being part of my life.

I would also like to thank my daughter Mickie. Without her help, I would not be where I am now.

To all my friends and family who supported me through their prayers and heartfelt thoughts, thank you all so much.

To all the people who are experiencing this kind of adversity, I am sharing my story with you with the hope that you will draw inspiration and courage from my experience and that there is always hope when you get a second chance in life.

Acknowledgment

To my husband, James, I want to express my deepest gratitude to you for being my awesome partner whom I trust, honor, and respect. You are an unwavering source of support and inspiration throughout the journey of writing this book. Your encouragement, patience, and understanding have been invaluable to me. I am endlessly grateful for your love and belief in my dreams. Thank you for standing by me at every step of the way.

To my dearest Daughter, Mickie, and Son, Miko; you two have been my greatest motivation and constant reminders of why I do what I do. Your boundless enthusiasm, endless hugs, and unwavering faith in me have fueled my determination to see this project through. Thank you for being my sunshine on even the cloudiest of days. I love you both more than words can express.

To my esteemed publisher's team: I extend my heartfelt appreciation to each and every one of you for your dedication, expertise, and unwavering commitment to bringing this book to fruition. Your guidance, professionalism, and passion for literature have been instrumental in shaping this project into what it is today. I am profoundly grateful for the opportunity to collaborate with such a talented and supportive team.

Thank you all for your unwavering support, love, and belief in me. This book would not have been possible without each and every one of you.

With deepest gratitude,

Imee R. Warren

Table of Contents

Preface

Chapter 1: Growing Up By The Sea—Imee's Family Tale

Chapter 2: Shadows And Sunshine Piercing The High School Maze

Chapter 3: Family Hullabaloo And Tough Choices

Chapter 4: Finding My Path

Chapter 5: Unexpected Beginnings

Chapter 6: Sailing Through The Storm

Chapter 7: Selling Success

Chapter 8: From Dreams To Departure

Chapter 9: A New Beginning In Oman

Chapter 10: Rising Tides of Reawakening

Chapter 11: The Shifting Sands of Life

Chapter 12: Striving to Bridge the Divide

Chapter 13: Breaking Illusions & Finding Reality

Chapter 14: Under The Blazing Sun

Chapter 15: A Pandemic Twist

Chapter 16: The Fire That Changed Everything

Chapter 17: Pain, Patience, and Perseverance

Chapter 18: Enduring the Agony

Chapter 19: Strength in the Season of Healing

Chapter 20: Embracing Life, One Trip at a Time

PREFACE

In the quiet moments before dawn, I often find myself reflecting on the journey that brought me here. A journey marked by fire—both the literal flames that engulfed my body and the metaphorical flames that ignited my spirit. At 41%, my skin bears the scars of survival, each one telling a story of resilience, pain, and, ultimately, rebirth. The day of the accident is etched in my memory with vivid clarity. The world felt surreal as I emerged from the chaos, my body a canvas of trauma, yet my heart remained unyielding. Those who have not walked this path may struggle to understand the depth of such an experience. But for me, it was a transformative awakening, forcing me to confront my fears and redefine my identity. This autobiography is not just a recounting of my scars; it is a testament to the strength of the human spirit. It explores the moments of vulnerability, the battles fought in silence, and the unwavering hope that carried me through the darkest times. As I share my story, I invite you to journey with me through the fire, into the depths of despair, and ultimately toward healing and empowerment. Through the pages that follow, you will find the lessons learned, the love discovered, and the unbreakable resolve that continues to shape my life. This is not just my story; it is a message to anyone who has ever felt consumed by their

Preface

circumstances. Together, let us rise from the ashes, stronger and more beautiful than before.

In the depths of despair, when shadows seemed to swallow every flicker of hope, I discovered an unshakeable truth: nothing is impossible to God. My journey began on a day that forever altered my life—a day when flames consumed not just my body but also the life I once knew. My scars are a testament to both suffering and survival. This autobiography is more than a chronicle of my physical and emotional battles; it is a celebration of divine grace and resilience. With every painful step toward recovery, I learned that true strength lies not in the absence of pain but in the courage to rise again, fueled by faith. As I share my story, I invite you to witness the power of belief and the miracles that unfold when we surrender our fears to a higher purpose. Each chapter reveals moments of doubt and despair but also extraordinary instances of love, support, and divine intervention.

Through the flames of my past, I have found a new life—a life dedicated to inspiring others to embrace their own journeys, no matter how daunting they may seem. Together, let us dare to believe that with faith and determination, anything is possible. This is not just my story; it is a call to all who struggle to remember that they are never alone and that within each of us lies the potential for incredible transformation.

CHAPTER 1
GROWING UP BY THE SEA— IMEE'S FAMILY TALE

In the fall of 1966, I was born in Manila into a not-so-wealthy family. By the time I was born, my father, a marine merchant, was already established in his profession. He operated locally, but despite this, he would be gone for upto six months at a time. As a result, my mother was the one in charge most of the time.

I am the only girl in my family, with four brothers. Unfortunately, one passed away back in 2018, leaving me with three brothers. My eldest brother and I share a close bond since we are only one year apart.

With so many brothers around, our house was always lively. We played games, argued, and looked out for each other. Sometimes, our house felt like a bustling playground, echoing with laughter and shouts. Our days were filled with childhood adventures and mischief.

My siblings and I were born in Manila. My father, however, was originally from Visaya, Mindanao province, which is in the northern part of the Philippines. In our house, our dialect was Tagalog. My father's native dialect was Visaya which he never taught us. Because of this, he

Chapter 1: Growing Up By The Sea—Imee's Family Tale

and his siblings would communicate with us in broken Tagalog or English. As for our family name, it is Retorta. I am of mixed heritage and do not have the typical physical appearance of a Filipino. I have many features that are more familiar to the Spaniards.

To give you an idea, I often use JLO as a reference point when trying to describe my appearance. I strive for confidence and elegance in presenting myself to the world. But like anyone, I harbor my own personal insecurities.

My mother comes from a large family, with three sisters and four brothers – that makes a total of eight siblings.

As the family's first and only daughter, I was treated as the favorite. My mother treated me like a doll – dressing me up, matching my shoes with my bag, and so on. This pampering has continued over the years. To this day, I am very meticulous about my appearance.

My father also adored me, calling me his princess and showering me with plenty of nice toys. His love and care wrapped around me like a warm hug, creating cherished memories that continue to brighten my days.

My paternal grandmother held a special place for me in her heart. She thoroughly enjoyed styling my hair and dressing me up elegantly. Her gentle touch and loving attention made me feel like the most special

Chapter 1: Growing Up By The Sea—Imee's Family Tale

grandchild in the world, leaving me with many cherished memories of her tender care.

My mother often shared with me that she felt that she missed out on qualities such as class and style. She sensed she lacked the elegance and grace my grandmother worked so hard to instill in me as I grew up.

Seeing the bond between my grandma and me weighed heavily on her heart, and she longed to embody those same qualities so she could have taught me instead of my grandmother.

What my mother did not realize was that her life's journey took a different path; she did not have the chance to complete high school, which meant she approached certain things with a different perspective. Even though she did not have a formal education, my mother's wisdom and love were boundless. In fact, it was her nurturing presence that helped guide me through many of life's ups and downs.

Education holds great importance in our family. Both my father and his siblings pursued their education diligently. I have two aunts who were teachers, and my father's older sister was a registered nurse. She worked for over 40 years until she died. Additionally, my father's eldest brother had a career as a chief nautical engineer.

I was born and raised in the same area where I attended school from elementary through high school. It was a local school, and at the time of my birth, the area was considered somewhat rough, akin to what you might think of a ghetto in Brooklyn, New York, or Chinatown in LA.

As I grew up, I witnessed lots of violence and chaos in our neighborhood. It started when I was about five and continued until I was seven. All this turmoil made me unsure of where I fit in. It was like the world around me was always on edge, and I did not know where I belonged in it.

The fights and riots were scary. Sometimes, they happened right outside our house, and we had to stay indoors until things calmed down. It made me wonder why people were so angry and why there was so much conflict. It also taught me to put on a strong face to show no fear.

My parents, especially my father's mother, were deeply religious, and their faith greatly influenced my upbringing. I was raised with strict religious discipline, following certain rituals and practices.

For instance, we would eat together as a family at the same time every day. We would gather for prayer, usually reciting the rosary at six o'clock each evening. Additionally, when it came to meals, we were expected to finish everything on our plates. Leaving food uneaten on a plate was prohibited in our household.

Outside of meal time, our playtime was also regulated. We had to finish playing by 5 or 5:30 in the evening and then shower. This discipline

Chapter 1: Growing Up By The Sea—Imee's Family Tale

and routine were instilled in us not only by our grandparents but also by our aunts and uncles. An example of this would be showing respect, "mano po," or placing our forehead on the back of their hand.

To sum it up, our family was very pious, and this commitment to faith influenced every aspect of our daily lives, instilling in us a strong sense of discipline and routine. Our mornings started with prayers, and our days were filled with teachings from the Bible. Our meals were occasions for gratitude, each one blessed before we began. Every decision we made, big or small, was guided by our beliefs. All of this helped to shape our personalities and how we interacted with the world around us.

As a young girl, when we misbehaved, our elders had a disciplinary method that left a lasting impression. If our aberration were significant, they would make us kneel down with our arms spread, holding books in both hands. For more serious offenses, they would have us kneel on a salt rack, which was very uncomfortable.

These disciplinary measures ingrained in me a deep fear of making mistakes. Ensuring I was careful in my actions to avoid such consequences. To this day, I will spend a lot of time considering an action or decision before acting on it.

As for my father, his job kept him away for most of the year. He would be gone for 11 months and only return home for a month before going back to work again. Due to his work schedule, I had very little

Chapter 1: Growing Up By The Sea—Imee's Family Tale

opportunity to spend time with him. However, during his brief visits home, he would emphasize the importance of education. His dedication to his job and commitment to our education were his clear priorities.

Growing up, I struggled with mathematics, and whenever my father came home, he would make it a point to check my homework. He would focus primarily on my math assignments. He would closely observe as I worked through the problems. If he found my performance lacking, he would discipline me by lightly hitting my hand with his flip-flops. These sessions often ended in tears.

There were times when I would reach a point where I did not want him to be at home due to the fear of facing his potential discipline. His presence in the house became associated with stress and anxiety, and I sometimes found relief in his absence.

Although my father was quite strict when it came to my education, there were also moments of warmth and affection. I remember times when I would sit next to him while watching TV. I also remember when he would playfully place me on his legs, pretending they were like a horse for me to ride.

These moments of playful interaction provided a sense of comfort and bonding between us, especially during my early childhood years when I was around five or six years old.

Chapter 1: Growing Up By The Sea—Imee's Family Tale

My father was extremely protective of me. He treated me like a delicate crystal and was concerned about my safety. When he was home, he rarely allowed me to go outside because he feared for my well-being. I was beautiful in his eyes, and he worried about all the potential dangers lurking outside.

We lived in a gated house, and my father's concern stemmed from the belief that he would not be able to protect me once I stepped beyond its confines. He was cautious of not knowing where I might go or what could happen to me out there.

In the Philippines, particularly where we lived, playing outside was generally considered safe, as there were few cars passing through residential areas. However, my father's protective nature often restricted my outdoor activities, as he prioritized my safety above all else. This over-protection could be very frustrating.

Despite our challenges, one constant source of joy was my father's thoughtful gestures whenever he returned home. I vividly recall one instance when I was around eight years old. He brought me a popular toy—a walking doll the same height as me. This doll was a cherished possession. It had a speaker in its belly, allowing it to talk, and its blonde hair was neatly braided on both sides. I loved sharing this doll with the other kids in the neighborhood. Whenever I took it out to play, it became a communal enjoyment, bringing smiles to all the children's faces.

Chapter 1: Growing Up By The Sea—Imee's Family Tale

Regardless of the hardships we faced, moments like these highlighted the simple joys and connections that transcended economic circumstances.

Living in a neighborhood with a squatter area or what would be called a ghetto nearby, our neighbors were not always well-off. My father was frequently away, so I felt closer to my mother and uncles. They were all very strict with me and my siblings, ensuring we followed the rules and upheld our responsibilities.

This one incident involving my uncle stands out in my memory. We had a wooden gate at our home that had a nail peeking out. Normally, when something broke, it was up to us, the owner, to fix it. There were no repair services like in the United States where someone would be called to repair it. Instead, we took matters into our own hands. In this case, nobody bothered to fix it. One day, while playing, I jumped and impaled my right hand on the nail. My uncle rushed out and lifted me off so I could free up my hand. Needless to say, the gate was soon repaired.

Growing up without sisters and being surrounded by four brothers, I naturally gravitated towards their activities and interests. As a result, I developed tomboyish conduct, preferring to participate in traditionally masculine pursuits rather than conforming to more feminine stereotypes.

As far as my clothing choices were concerned, I avoided dresses in favor of practical and comfortable attire, often opting for very short

Chapter 1: Growing Up By The Sea—Imee's Family Tale

shorts. My behavior earned me the nickname "Maldita," which means spoiled brat in English, reflecting my independent and adventurous spirit.

Whether it was joining in on their games or simply being part of their circle, I always made sure to assert my presence and being included in whatever they were doing.

My mother held a special status among her siblings because she was financially better-off. Two of my mother's younger brothers lived with us. Though they were older than us, they were still relatively young. Around 10 to 15 years older than me and my brother.

We had two maids in our household, and their daily routine included preparing breakfast for the family. However, I had a habit of expressing my displeasure with the breakfast options.

Each morning, I would wake up and intentionally make a noise by dragging my feet as I made my way downstairs to the staircase's landing.

My mother would notice this behavior and ask me about it, knowing full well that breakfast was already set on the table. My reluctance to eat the prepared breakfast made me a bit of a difficult child in that regard. I would often have them prepare something else of my choosing.

Chapter 1: Growing Up By The Sea—Imee's Family Tale

Growing up, I was quite a naughty girl and, admittedly, very spoiled. I never learned how to cook, as our maids prepared our meal, as it was the custom, five times a day.

When my father came home, tensions arose over what to watch on TV. My brothers would have their preferences, but if I did not like what they chose, I would assert my own choice by changing the channel. Surprisingly, my father would change the channel to my preference without any objections.

Moving on, I was considered a popular girl at school. Partly because of the way I dressed, I would get a new uniform every year. Moreover, if there was a trendy shoe that everyone wanted, I would always be the first to have it. Getting that shoe or accessory became a passion of mine. I wanted to fit in and be seen as fashionable among my peers.

I have a best friend named Nancy, who remains a dear friend to this day. Despite our strong bond, there was a stark contrast in our economic situation. Nancy's family was always struggling financially and often faced challenges like not having enough food to eat.

Back in school, I clearly remember Nancy's uniform would show wear and tear because it was the only one she had. The school uniform consisted of a white top and a green skirt, with added lines for each subsequent year. Nancy's circumstances highlighted the difference in our lives, a realization that has always stayed with me.

Chapter 1: Growing Up By The Sea—Imee's Family Tale

To help my friend, I took matters into my own hands. Whenever I received a new uniform or pair of shoes, I would give her my old ones, even if they may have been slightly worn. I knew they would be of great value to her.

Nancy would adjust the uniforms to fit her size and make any necessary repairs to ensure they looked presentable. As for the shoes, I would intentionally wear them out just enough to make them seem undesirable to me. Then, I would ask my mother for a new pair, and once I received them, I would give the slightly worn ones to Nancy.

In this way, I found a small but meaningful way to support my friend, ensuring she had the essentials she needed for school despite her family's financial struggles.

Reflecting on my childhood, I often ponder the extent to which it has shaped the person I am today. To answer this question, I turn to my father. He was a man of strong principles, constantly imparting wisdom as I grew up. He always stressed the importance of having dreams and ambitions in life. He also emphasized the need for one's abilities to match those ambitions. He taught me the value of integrity, always insisting that you must stand by your word.

His teachings have profoundly impacted me, imparting a sense of resilience and determination. I still carry his words with me, believing nothing is impossible if one truly desires it. His emphasis on honor and

Chapter 1: Growing Up By The Sea—Imee's Family Tale

integrity has become ingrained in my character, influencing my actions and decisions to this day.

Reflecting on my journey, I realize I have become like my father in many ways. I work diligently, mindful of my reputation, just as he did. Even though he is not physically present, his teachings continue to guide me, constantly reminding me of the values he instilled in me.

CHAPTER 2
SHADOWS AND SUNSHINE PIERCING THE HIGH SCHOOL MAZE

In high school, I was somewhat popular because of my older brother. We all went to the same school, and our family name was well-known there. This resulted in me having a lot of friends, especially with the cool kids. Most of my friends were in the higher sections of my grade.

When I was in high school, we did not have a lot of money. My father worked as a Merchant Marine. He was the First Merchant Engineer on a cargo ship. Because of his job, I was introduced to many things like the Nivea, Oil of Olay, and even fancy perfumes like Chanel No. 5. Whenever he returned home, he would bring these as gifts, so I learned about them from a young age.

In high school, whenever something new or trendy came out, like Hello Kitty or My Melody, I already had it. That is one of the reasons I was popular and always ahead of the trends!

Back when everyone wore long skirts for the school uniform, I stood out by wearing short skirts. I was not like one of the mean girls, I was

Chapter 2: Shadows And Sunshine Piercing The High School Maze

popular because I was nice, and everyone wanted to be my friend. For example, if any student did not have lunch money, I would always share something with them.

There were also times when I did not have money myself. So, what did I do? I would ask other students for a few cents, gather it, and then share it with those who needed it. That is one of the reasons I became popular - I was always friendly and caring.

Whenever a friend wanted to borrow clothes, I would invite them over and let them pick something they liked from my wardrobe. I was super generous with everyone. I trusted people easily, and my reputation in school meant a lot to me.

When I was fourteen, I was friends with a group of gay guys (Bakla). In my country, there are many gay people, and I had four gay friends, of which three have since passed away. One remains my friend to this day, but unfortunately, we hardly talk to each other anymore.

My gay friends would come to me whenever they needed something or wanted attention from someone they liked, whether it was a boy or a girl. But one day, something changed, and I can not quite recall what it was. But whatever it was, my gay friends were not very happy with me.

They began spreading rumors about me, claiming I was not a virgin anymore. I was only fourteen! It was incredibly hurtful and made me feel

Chapter 2: Shadows And Sunshine Piercing The High School Maze

really low. Everyone began to gossip about it, and it became a big deal at school. The rumors made me feel judged and isolated. It was difficult to escape the whispers and stares. It was a challenging period where I felt misunderstood and unfairly targeted by others' opinions and judgments. It was the first time that I realized how hurtful words and simple actions could be.

I was hurt and puzzled, trying to figure out what I had done to make them so angry with me. Out of nowhere, they started acting distant and even displayed open anger at me. I struggled to understand why and how to deal with it, and I felt like I was walking on eggshells around them, not knowing what I had done or how to fix it. Their sudden change in attitude left me feeling isolated and depressed. Fourteen is a tough age, anyway. Then, trying to cope with those emotions and figuring out how to deal with them created tremendous stress that I was not equipped to handle.

Feeling overwhelmed and not knowing how to cope, I took a drastic step. I attempted suicide! My father always had these soft gel vitamin E capsules that he kept in the fridge. In a moment of despair, I took the entire bottle, about 100 or 150 capsules, and swallowed them all. It was a desperate act, and I did not really think about the consequences at that moment. I just wanted the pain and confusion to stop, and this was the only way I could think of that would end my pain and humiliation.

Chapter 2: Shadows And Sunshine Piercing The High School Maze

After taking all those capsules, I blacked out, and my father found me unconscious on the floor. He was terrified and immediately rushed me to the emergency room. He was crying and kept asking me why I would do such a thing.

At the hospital, they inserted a tube into my stomach to pump it out. I recall seeing a large glass bottle hanging on a pole, flushing my stomach. They used this method to pump my stomach; first, they ran the fluid in and then suck it back out. It took five of those bottles to clear out everything I had taken. My stomach contents were initially a dark liquid, and they did not stop until it became clear to ensure they removed everything.

After that scary incident, everyone at home was shaken up and concerned about me. They were upset by the incident and never knew why I did what I did. They never talked to me or asked me about it. They never question my piousness or my motive. I kept the real reason to myself; I did not share it with anyone. My father and my brothers never knew why I attempted suicide.

My Catholic upbringing played a significant role in the stigma surrounding the rumors about my virginity. Back then and even now, people are very traditional and conservative. My family was religious and conservative, too. In my hometown, people place a lot of importance on the teachings of the church, and waiting until marriage before being

Chapter 2: Shadows And Sunshine Piercing The High School Maze

intimate was one of them. There is a tradition of wearing a white wedding gown and walking down the church aisle. This was reserved for those who have chosen to wait until marriage. That is how strict it is. Because of this, I was bullied, and my reputation suffered. My father would have been very upset if he thought I had shared that part of myself. Chastity is highly valued in my country, even today. Many girls feel it is imperative to maintain their purity until marriage.

In other countries, dating might include being intimate with someone, but in my culture, it is different. Sleeping with someone is seen as something you do only with the person you will marry. You can not be with any other men. This mindset was deeply ingrained in me during my upbringing.

Being a woman in my culture meant that only the man you marry should touch you or be intimate with you. My morality and values were shaped by these beliefs, making my virginity very important to me and my community.

It is natural to wonder if there was anyone who could have supported me through the bullying and rumors I was facing. The truth is, when the rumors started, everyone believed them. No one questioned the truth of the rumors. Through this ordeal, I realized how true a "mob" mentality really is.

Chapter 2: Shadows And Sunshine Piercing The High School Maze

I felt so embarrassed and ashamed about something I never did that I did not want to see anyone. It felt like a "walk of shame" whenever I had to face other people back then. Even if someone tried to help or support me, I would not let them. I did not talk to my brothers about it, and none of my friends were supportive. They unquestioningly believed the rumors, too.

Back then, we did not have cell phones or social media to reach out to friends so easily. The only way to communicate was through letters or face to face. I isolated myself and stopped going to school. I kept everything to myself. I was too embarrassed to show my face or talk with anyone. As a result, even if there were people who could have helped, I did not let them because of how I felt alone and isolated from the world.

As the rumors spread, I could not bring myself to go to school. It took weeks for the rumors to end. These friends of mine, who I had dearly loved and trusted, were the ones spreading it. They were funny and popular, and I thought they were close to me. One of them even shared the same birthday as me. I could not believe that they would do this to me. After the rumor reached every ear in the school, it was difficult for me to go back there and meet eyes with them.

As you may have already realized, I am naturally quite sensitive. I also tend to keep everything inside me when a challenging time comes my way. Most people around me do not even realize I am struggling until

Chapter 2: Shadows And Sunshine Piercing The High School Maze

I have sorted things out and moved past them. I have never been one to share my struggles openly because I do not want to weigh others down and have them feel pity for me. I have always been the one to manage my affairs alone, and I only open up when I have already come through the other side and feel okay again. It is just how I have coped and maintained my independence.

When I attempted suicide, I saw the different reactions of my parents. They did not know why I took such an extreme step, but they knew something was not right. Their different reactions showed me how people can handle difficult situations in different ways, but deep down, they both loved and cared about me—wanting only the best for me, even if they expressed it differently.

My father did not know about the rumors since they were confined to the school. My brothers knew about them but never brought them up with me. They knew the rumors were not true because I did not have a boyfriend and was not dating anyone.

My father was there with me at the hospital. In the emergency room, before any treatment began, he asked me straight up if I was pregnant. It was such a shocking question to hear from my father, as I was actually too young to get pregnant. However, I felt that even if I was, he would still have accepted and supported me. I know he would have been hurt. You see, family reputation and honor were very important to him. Despite

Chapter 2: Shadows And Sunshine Piercing The High School Maze

this, I know he would have stood by me and was always very protective of me.

My mother reacted differently. She was aware of the rumors, and I felt like she believed them, or maybe she was just disappointed in me that I could have been intimate with someone. Our mentalities were very different. My mother always had this feeling that I was doing something behind her back. I loved my mother dearly, but our relationship was like oil and water. We just did not see eye to eye on many things, and to think she would believe those rumors and not trust her own daughter was very hurtful.

Being the only girl in the family, I often felt like I competed with her. I remember her disapproving of me going out. I felt like I had to sneak out of the house. There was one time, a particularly tough time, she even threatened to chain me to the staircase when she caught me doing something rebellious. She said things to scare me, but I was not easily frightened. I am strong-willed, not easily controlled, like an Iron Woman, but I am also emotional, sensitive, and can easily be hurt.

It is through episodes like these that I have realized that our minds have much more power than our hearts and feelings. I have had to train myself to think things through logically and use my brain to make choices instead of running with my first emotion.

Chapter 2: Shadows And Sunshine Piercing The High School Maze

Living through all these ups and downs in life has toughened me up. I have found that I do not get as easily upset or affected by things as I used to. Now, I bounce back from setbacks more quickly and can handle whatever comes my way with a stronger attitude.

Eventually, all my friends who had been spreading rumors felt guilty about what they had done to me and the aftermath of their actions. They eventually apologized, and after that, things began to improve. Even though it was a lot to handle at such a young age, I knew moving on with my life and forgiving my friends was the only way to keep myself sane.

My father did not get angry or overly upset when he asked me about the situation. I was crying but could not bring myself to tell him the truth. Instead, I made up a story about not being happy without revealing the real issue. I was afraid that if my father found out about the rumors and my friends' involvement, he would stop them from coming to our house. Yet, despite the rumors, my best friends did come over, showing that my parents were supportive and understanding.

My parents have always been there for me, even if they did not know the full extent of what I was going through. They were supportive in their own way, trying to understand and help me through the tough times.

In the whirlwind of high school popularity and cultural expectations, I faced some of the toughest challenges of my young life. From being the

Chapter 2: Shadows And Sunshine Piercing The High School Maze

trendsetter with a heart of gold to grappling with hurtful rumors and the weight of my cultural background, I learned resilience the hard way.

While it felt like the world was against me at times, my family's support, in their own unique ways, became my anchor.

It was not always smooth sailing; misunderstandings, clashes, and personal battles tested me. Yet, reflecting on those turbulent years, I realize they shaped the strong, independent woman I am today.

Through highs and lows, family ties, and cultural norms, I found my path, learning that true strength lies in accepting who you are, standing by your values, and cherishing those who stand by you, no matter what.

CHAPTER 3
FAMILY HULLABALOO AND TOUGH CHOICES

Life can be unpredictable and often throws unexpected curveballs. Among all my experiences, one particular incident really shook me to the core. It was a time when I saw my family falling apart; this changed everything for me. While I do not know how my brothers felt about it, for me, it was a pivotal moment that led to my rebellious phase.

I felt lost and did not know how to handle the situation. I did not want others to know that our family was struggling... struggling to stay a family. High school was behind me. With whatever happened to me with all the rumors, I never found enough courage to go back to that place and face everyone. What was even worse was that I altogether stopped taking classes and as a matter of fact, got far away from studying. I even lied to my parents and told them I was going to take the classes. I simply went to my friend's house to hang out and have fun.

I did not choose to be a rebellious person. The situation at home transformed me into such a person. It was not like I woke up one day and decided to break the rules; the change was very gradual.

Chapter 3: Family Hullabaloo And Tough Choices

My family was striving to stay together, but I could see that it was falling apart. Even the thought of my family drifting apart took my stress to a whole other level of experiencing pain and confusion. I honestly struggled to cope with the changes and uncertainties it brought into our lives. I felt like the ground beneath me was shifting, and I did not know how to find my footing again. Those feelings of despair and hopelessness became overwhelming, and I found myself questioning many things, including my worth and my place within the family.

In 1983, when I was seventeen, things got pretty intense. Trying to juggle my personal life and family drama was not easy. It felt like a big deal back then, and looking back, it still feels like a crossroad in my life. One day, my grandma dropped a bombshell on me. She spilled the beans about what was really going on between my parents. Turns out, while Father was away on his ship in Spain, he got close to another woman. It was a shock to hear. Grandma said he almost decided to stay with her instead of coming back to us. I found this hard to believe, as it was a lot for me to take in at the time.

Learning this was like having the rug pulled out from under me. It was hard to wrap my head around the idea that my father could consider leaving our family for someone else. The thought of it was unsettling and brought up so many emotions like anger, sadness, and betrayal.

Chapter 3: Family Hullabaloo And Tough Choices

This revelation explained the tension and strain I had been feeling at home, but it also added a layer of complexity to my feelings towards my father. I struggled to reconcile my image of him as a loving father with this new information. It was a lot to process, and it definitely contributed to the reason I become to defy my parents and their rules.

Coming to terms with this new reality was a long and challenging journey. It took time for me to find a way to understand and accept what was happening while also trying to heal and rebuild trust within my family.

Eventually, my father did return home. When he came back, burdened by guilt, he confessed to my mother about the affair and his feelings for the other woman. It was a painful revelation for her and a betrayal of trust that deeply affected our family.

This incident was a major factor in creating tension within our family that I witnessed growing up. It explained a lot about the challenges we faced during that time. It was hard for me to process this information, knowing that my family was crumbling all because of my father's actions.

I felt like the ground beneath me was constantly shifting. I was caught in the middle of this family crisis and I did not know how to navigate it. The betrayal and its aftermath affected not just my parents' relationship but also the trust and stability within the entire family unit. It also profoundly affected my relationship with my father.

Chapter 3: Family Hullabaloo And Tough Choices

It was a lot for me to handle, especially while coping with the transition from high school to college—child to adult.

A lot of ups and downs marked this period of my life as I tried to find my way and figure out who I was amidst all the chaos. It was a challenging time of growth and self-discovery. While it was incredibly tough, it also played a pivotal role in shaping me into the person I am today.

This time in my life was incredibly hard for me, but what my mother was going through was ever harder. Knowing that your husband was having an affair with someone else while he was away for work is truly earth-shattering for any woman. Though my mother never talked to me about it, I know it was the same for her as well. I know it because after learning about the affair, she could not forgive my father. The trust that had once been the bedrock of their relationship was shattered. Our family dynamic changed forever. I could feel the tension and watch the distance growing between my parents. This impacted our entire family, resulting in all of us creating boundaries between each other.

The memory of my father coming home after my mother learned the truth about his affair is still vivid in my eyes. I remember him bringing home gifts for us—shoes, clothes, perfume—but my mother could not bear to keep them. She gathered everything together, poured gasoline

Chapter 3: Family Hullabaloo And Tough Choices

over them, and set them on fire. It was a symbolic act, showing her anger and pain of being betrayed.

We could only feel two atmospheres under our roof—either it was heavy with silence or filled with arguments. One memory that stands out powerfully is seeing my mother holding two bottles of Mateus Rose Wine. The bottles are distinctive, with a unique-green-oval shape. I thought they were champagne, but it was actually a Portuguese Rose wine. She took those bottles and locked herself and my youngest brother, Jimmy, in the back bedroom while my father was on the other side of the door, pleading and yelling for forgiveness.

It was a heartbreaking scene, and these memories are etched in my mind. The pain and the emotional turmoil that our family went through during that time had a lasting impact on me.

From then on, my mother was really tough on my father. Constantly pushing his buttons and making life hard for him. Even though she never left him, their life together was full of struggles and our home was never the same again.

My mother was religious and believed that once two people are married, nothing should tear them apart. She often said, "What God has joined together, let no one separate." That was why they stayed together, even though their life was strained right up to the end.

Chapter 3: Family Hullabaloo And Tough Choices

From that time until my mother passed away three years ago, she never forgave my father. He passed away in 2014 without ever getting forgiveness from her. This is a true story from my life, and it feels hurtful to think about to this day.

It is from my experience that I have learned how important trust is in a relationship. Without trust, you can never fully give yourself to another and never truly love them.

CHAPTER 4
FINDING MY PATH

After everything that happened at home, my father stopped working. Since we did not have much money, my parents could not afford to send me and my eldest brother to college. Fortunately, my mother's brother, who was better-off, offered his help despite already having a big family of his own. He owned a convenience store and a small restaurant which provided him a steady income. It was a relief for my mother when he offered to help us. My uncle recognized our situation and understood that we needed his support so we could continue our schooling. As a result, my mother decided that she should send me and my brother Conrad to stay with my uncle.

Unfortunately, things did not work out the way we thought they would. Instead of helping us with school as he promised, he had us help him open, close, and work as a cashier in the restaurant. We were also responsible for the upkeep of the house. It was quite troubling. We stayed there for almost a month and instead of him helping us, we helped him. When my father learned about this sad situation that we were in, he decided to bring me and my brother back home. He also hoped that bringing us back would help resolve some of the tension and issues within our family. However, by that point, I had already become rebellious. I was deeply unhappy with everything that was going on, and I felt helpless to change the situation.

Returning back home did not fix anything for me. It felt more like going back to a place where problems, issues and attitudes were still in the air, and everyone was feeling stressed. I was annoyed with everything that was happening and felt stuck, as if there was no way out of the mess that was our family. I started behaving in an unruly way because I was so unhappy. I was not equipped to deal with all the emotions inside me. I started acting out and resisted doing what people expected from me. I felt like I did not belong and I could not meet everyone's expectations.

My brother and I were still not enrolled in any school, let alone college. We were not getting any type of education. Fortunately, my father's older brother, who was a chief engineer on a cargo ship, offered to help and agreed to send me and my brother to college. My brothers were sent to a public college, while I ended up going to a Catholic school called Letran college. It was a good fit because everyone from the professors to the administration was made up of priests and nuns and the environment was very structured.

That was back in 1983, when I was just starting my first year of college. During that summer, I had become quite a non-conformist, living life on my own terms. Instead of going to school like I was supposed to, I would pretend to go, but then I would pack my clothes and spend time

Chapter 4: Finding My Path

with my friends instead. We would skip classes and go to hang out at the coffee shop, fast food places and my favorite afternoon disco club.

We often went to afternoon discos where many college students went to dance and have fun. I enjoyed going there too. However, I had to change out of my school uniform before entering because they did not allow students wearing uniforms inside bars or clubs and besides, these clothes were not "cool."

As time went on, I began to act out and my behavior became worse. I started telling lies to my parents. I would ask them for money to pay my school fees, but instead of using it for its intended purpose, I kept it for myself. To cover up my lies, I went as far as creating fake receipts to show them, pretending that I had paid the fees. I continued deceiving my parents for as long as I could. They never suspected anything. Mother would watch me leave for school every day, unaware of my deception, while Father resumed his work without suspecting anything was wrong.

I found it hard to focus on anything besides spending time with my friends. Every day, I would leave home pretending to go to school, but I would end up just hanging out with my friends. During that time, I did not feel like studying or doing anything useful. It was as if my mind decided to make a new rule or goal to do things that would make my parents unhappy.

Chapter 4: Finding My Path

When it came to getting into university, I faced a bit of a problem. You see, universities base their decision on how well you did in your classes. If you got good grades and such, they would accept you. As a result of my behavior, things got a bit tricky. During this phase in my life, I did not study much, and my grades were not as they should have been. This made it harder for me when I started applying to a good university.

Even though I acted like a perfect student to my parents and everyone else, the reality was different. I would enroll at the start of each semester, get my uniform, and even show up for the first few days of class. I made it seem like everything was going well, even though deep down, I was struggling.

I acted like everything was fine and even my brothers did not suspect anything wrong. I really wanted my parents to think I was a good girl like I was doing everything right, even though secretly, I was neglecting my classes.

I was not really the "good girl" everyone thought I was. Yes, I put on a good act, pretending to be responsible and diligent, but the reality was quite different. In addition to spending time with my friends, I also started smoking and drinking, things that a "good girl" would not typically do. And even on the days when I did manage to drag myself to class, I did not actually go to my classes. Instead, I would wander around the campus aimlessly, not really engaging in anything meaningful or productive.

Chapter 4: Finding My Path

Back in 1983, I had a lot of freedom to go out because of what was happening in the country. You see, it was the time Ninoy Aquino was assassinated, and the whole country was in turmoil. People were unhappy and started protesting against the government. It was a huge thing that was happening right there in my country!

Because of all this protesting and rallying, schools often had to be suspended in Metro Manila. My mother always thought going to school was really important, but she did not know that classes had been suspended during that time.

The year 1983 was a year to remember. When I think about it now, I realize that these challenges helped me become stronger. That year was filled with so many crazy things happening, and I had to face a lot of changes. When I look back on those days, I can see how much they helped to shape me into the person I am today.

After all of this confusion and chaos, I began to understand more about myself and how it shaped me. On the outside, I acted like everything was okay, but on the inside, I was struggling. I realized that I needed to make peace with both parts of myself as I grew into an adult. It was like I had to accept and understand all the different sides of who I was becoming.

In the middle of all these changes, I took some time to think deeply about who I really was. I had to let go of what other people expected from

Chapter 4: Finding My Path

me and face my own worries and uncertainties. It felt like I was shining a light on the parts of myself that I did not want to see. I was able to confront my fears and explore my thoughts to better understand myself. It was scary, but I believed it would help me stay true to who I am.

With each step, I learned new things about myself, even those parts that I was not so fond of. Those tough times left their mark on me, but they also made me stronger. They reminded me that I can overcome any obstacle that comes my way. I will always carry memories of those challenging times. They have played a part in shaping me into the person I am today and they are a part of me.

CHAPTER 5
UNEXPECTED BEGINNINGS

In high school, I did not experience falling in love or having a boyfriend due to the rumors about me. Innuendo made me not want to think about being in a relationship. But when I started college in the second semester, things changed. I began to see things differently.

After starting my second semester of college, friends convinced me to check out a popular spot known for its lively atmosphere—a daytime disco. This was a place where students from various colleges and private universities in my area would hang out. It was there that I met a guy similar to my age, perhaps 17 or 18. His name was Perry. Despite the challenges I was facing in school and my lack of previous romantic experiences, I found myself drawn to him. There was something about his appearance and bearing that captivated me. I felt a connection that I had never experienced before. It was a new and exciting feeling, one that filled me with both anticipation and uncertainty.

He was very good-looking; he was taller than a typical Filipino with fair skin and dark brown hair. I could not stop thinking about the idea of someone like him liking me. I was a nobody from a small town, and

Chapter 5: Unexpected Beginnings

getting attention from him meant a lot to me. So, when he asked me to hang out with him, I said yes without hesitation.

I was only 18 when we slept together for the first time. This made me feel really special. But my mother did not approve of him. In our culture, it was not okay for a man and a woman to sleep together before they are married. She did not want us to be together like that. Because of my mother's disapproval, we ran away together. For the next month or so we would crash at the houses of various friends. Perry's father was a local judge, and because of our absence, he started searching for us. With the help of my parents, they located us. Perry's father did not approve of our relationship. I was returned to my home and Perry's to his. This lasted only two days and Perry showed up at my house. It was here that he stayed for the next month.

Even though my mother disagreed, he stayed with me in our home. Here, we lived as if we were husband and wife.

When we were together in bed, I thought it would be full of love. But instead, he did something strange. He would bite me all over, and it was really weird and also very painful. He bit me on my arms and legs, everywhere. I remember getting bruises all over. For him, it was funny, but for me, it hurt and I did not understand why. He bit me in places that were really sensitive, like under my arm and on my thigh. Sometimes, when I wore shorts, my mother would see the bites and bruises and ask

Chapter 5: Unexpected Beginnings

me about them. When I told her what they were, she would just smile and walk away. I cried a lot because it hurt so much. He did not hit me, but his biting made me want to scream. He would also tickle me so hard that I eventually ended up peeing myself. This was his twisted idea of fun. One day, when I could not take it anymore, so I told him to leave. We were together at my mother's house for about a month. After that, I told my mother I could not handle it anymore. I asked him to leave because I did not want to get hurt anymore.

I lost my virginity to Perry, but you know some relationships in life are not meant to be. And this relationship was one of those. I could say that he emotionally kidnapped me in a way.

After I asked him to leave, I missed my period and started having nausea and vomiting. I did not know what was going on. Then, one morning, I felt dizzy, and my mother saw something was wrong. That was when she figured out I was pregnant. Everything happened so fast, and I was scared. I did not know what to do or how to handle it. It was a confusing and overwhelming time for me. Fortunately, my mother supported and helped me through this life-altering event.

In our culture, having a baby before getting married is frowned upon, and at 18 years I was ill-equipped to deal with this situation.

I was with Perry for a few months and it was after he left that I found out I was pregnant. Perry and his family did not want anything to do with

Chapter 5: Unexpected Beginnings

my baby. I felt like a doll he was done playing with. His parents said, "We are not going to marry her to our son. She and her baby are your problem." Perry and his family did not want to accept any responsibility for my baby.

I was left crying, and my mother had to take care of me. So there I was, pregnant with no husband, feeling lost and scared.

I was eventually kicked out of my university. It was a Catholic school, and they did not allow unwed mothers to attend the school. Even though I was forced to leave the university, my father wanted me to keep studying. He found another school for me, which was an exclusive modeling school called Karilagan. This school was different because many famous people and celebrities attended here. It was also a place where you could learn to be a model. They allowed pregnant women to attend, but it cost a lot of money.

I went to classes there, trying to catch up on what I missed at the university. But my belly was getting bigger, and soon, my baby would be born. As a result, I did not finish my studies there.

During my time at Karilagan, I made a new friend who became my best friend. When I went out to do my errands, like shopping at the market, I would bump into people I knew from high school. Because I was well-known in town, they would gossip about me being pregnant without a husband. Hearing their whispers hurt, especially because I was

Chapter 5: Unexpected Beginnings

young. But I did not let this bring me down. I had too many challenges in my life to let what others said bother me too much. Instead, I focused on facing every problem that came my way. This strength helped me keep going, even when things moving forward seemed impossible.

In March of 1985, I found myself going into labor. It was a challenging moment, and I only had my mother at my side. I had no one else to offer me support. Instead of heading to a hospital, my mother opted to take me to a maternity clinic. She feared the shame and embarrassment our family might face due to my pregnancy without a husband, as it had already stirred up gossip and tarnished our reputation.

As I experienced labor pains at the clinic, I felt overwhelmed by the intensity of the situation. With no one to share my agony, I grappled with a whirlwind of emotions and thoughts. The pain was unbearable, prompting me to seek solace in the bathroom repeatedly.

In the confines of the bathroom, I found myself caught in a cycle of tears, screams, and prayers, desperately seeking respite from the relentless pain. It was a solitary struggle, with each passing moment feeling like an eternity. Despite my mother eventually joining me, I had already endured two days of labor, grappling with the physical and emotional toll it exacted.

During that time, pain relief options like those available in the United States were not accessible. I had to endure the pain alone. The medical

Chapter 5: Unexpected Beginnings

staff eventually had me lie down to assess my progress in labor. They found that my delivery was complicated because my water was not yet broken.

The pain was unbearable, and I feared for my life. I questioned whether what I was experiencing was normal. Being young and inexperienced, this was all foreign to me. I felt utterly isolated, facing the daunting task of giving birth alone. The absence of pain relief and protracted labor made the situation even more challenging. I had no choice but to endure the intense pain and uncertainty of childbirth.

When my baby girl was born in March 1985, my mother was not even in the room. I was all alone, fighting the intense pain of childbirth. It was not until after the birth that my mother finally arrived. My daughter, Mickie, never got to know her father because Perry passed away when she was only three years old. I took her to his funeral, but that is the only memory she has of him. I do not even have any photographs to remember him by. Now, at 39 years old, Mickie does not have a single picture or memory of her father.

Having my daughter changed everything for me; life took a new meaning. She became the best thing that ever happened to me. It did not matter what people said about me or that I was only 19 years old and a single mother. Despite the challenges, I was determined to take care of my baby girl all by myself.

Chapter 5: Unexpected Beginnings

As Mickie grew up, she became my whole world. I devoted myself entirely to her. From the moment she was born, I made a promise to myself that Mickie would not face the same struggles I did. Everything I would do would be for my children. I have lived by that promise until this very day, and I swear to God I continue to do so for my children and my five grandchildren.

CHAPTER 6
SAILING THROUGH THE STORM

In the neighborhood where I lived, there was a man who stood out from the rest. His name was Lito, he was quiet and kind. Someone who had a special interest in me. At that time, I was just a young woman of 21 years, carrying the responsibilities of a single mother. Despite the challenges that came with my situation, Lito looked beyond them and showed a genuine liking towards me.

I often found myself lost in thought, thinking of him. He was a contrast to Perry, softer and more caring towards me. Given the fact that I was a single mother, I worried that I needed a partner in life. Getting married would be a significant change, a positive one, especially considering my daughter's future.

In my country, there is a strict rule that is hard to ignore. The rule states that children who are born out of wedlock are not allowed admission to Catholic schools. This rule is non-negotiable and is strictly adhered to. Being a mother naturally made me worry about my daughter's education.

The thought of my daughter being denied education due to her birth circumstances was unsettling, to say the least. It made me realize that

Chapter 6: Sailing Through The Storm

marriage is not just a societal norm, it also is a crucial factor that could directly impact my daughter's future. This realization brought a new perspective to my life and the decisions I needed to make for the sake of my child's future. It was a challenging time. It also made me understand the complexities of life and the importance of making choices that could impact not only my life but also the future of my family.

As the days turned into weeks and the weeks into months, Lito, who had shown interest in me, gathered enough courage to express his feelings. He confessed that he had developed a deep affection for me. As I reflected on my own emotions, I realized that I too had grown fond of him. We started seeing each other more often, and our bond strengthened. In the beginning of 1987, we decided it was time to tie the knot. We had a simple ceremony at City Hall, marking the beginning of our journey as husband and wife.

Not long after our wedding, I discovered that I was pregnant once again. It was a joyous moment, knowing that our family was growing. Mickie would soon be a big sister.

During this time, we lived with my parents in my childhood home. Despite being a young mother and expecting my second child, I did not let my personal circumstances deter me from pursuing my education. I was determined to complete my studies and provide a better future for my children. My days were filled with studying, taking care of my daughter,

Chapter 6: Sailing Through The Storm

and managing household chores. I did my best to support my father, who had been a pillar of strength for all of us.

Lito had not completed his college education and did not have a steady job. He struggled to find his footing and we were not in a position to live independently as a family yet. Recognizing our struggles, my father stepped in, offering guidance and support as we navigated through these challenging circumstances. His wisdom and patience were invaluable during this phase of our lives. His unwavering support gave us the strength to face our challenges and work towards building a better future for our family.

As time passed, I became frustrated and embarrassed. Here I was, pregnant with my second child, yet still residing in my parents' home. Despite this, I was determined to improve our situation and supported my husband in every possible way.

As my pregnancy progressed, the responsibility of providing for my family fell heavily on me. Every morning, without fail, I would wake up at 4:30 and head to the local market by Jeepney. This task became increasingly challenging as my pregnancy progressed and the typical symptoms of nausea and fatigue kicked in. I did not let these challenges deter me. I was determined to do my part for my family.

At the market, I would negotiate with vendors for items like fruits and vegetables. I would frequently purchase long stock of bananas. These

Chapter 6: Sailing Through The Storm

were not just a fruit for us; they were a means of survival. I would transform them into a dessert called "saging con yelo," a traditional Filipino dessert.

Transporting the heavy grocery bags back home was another challenge. Our country relies on Jeepneys, tricycles, and sidecars (three-wheeled bicycles) for commuting and navigating the city. Pregnant and with my hands full of groceries, riding in one of these was quite an adventure. But no matter how daunting the task, I was able to push through and I would ride in a tricycle or three-wheeled bicycle home. I knew that every banana I brought home, every dish I cooked, was a step towards a better future for my family.

By the time the first rays of dawn were breaking, around 5:30 a.m., I would make my way back home. Without wasting a moment, I would dive straight into my next task - cooking. I prepared a variety of dishes, including "saging con yelo," a dessert made from bananas, and "pancit," a Filipino noodle dish that holds a special place in our country's cuisine. In addition to these, I also made a hearty noodle soup.

I set up a makeshift stall just outside our house, transforming our humble abode into a small breakfast spot for the neighborhood. Local children on their way to school and passersby would stop to enjoy a warm, home-cooked meal. Despite the early hours and the hard work, the sight of people enjoying the food I prepared was incredibly rewarding.

Chapter 6: Sailing Through The Storm

My determination was fueled by a significant reason. Even though my parents had provided us with a small studio next to their house, I was driven by a strong sense of self-reliance. My pride prevented me from asking them for anything, even basic necessities like milk for my children.

I decided to take matters into my own hands. I was determined to provide for my family independently to ensure that my children had everything they needed. I found something to sell, turning my cooking skills into a source of income.

September 1987, we were blessed with a baby boy, who we lovingly named Mico. Our family was now complete with two beautiful children. Despite all the challenges, it was a journey that I would be willing to undertake again for the sake of my loved ones. Every obstacle was just another hurdle to overcome on this journey of resilience and determination.

I kept my struggles hidden from my parents, especially my mother. I did not want them to worry or feel obligated to help. Whenever my mother asked if we had enough milk for the children, I would assure her that we did, even if that was not always the case. It was a small lie, but it was a lie born out of pride and a fierce desire to be independent. This was my journey, a testament to resilience, determination, and the lengths a mother will go to ensure the well-being of her family.

Chapter 6: Sailing Through The Storm

Living with my parents was challenging, particularly with my mother's constant criticism. It felt like no matter what I did, it was never good enough for her. Instead of offering help or advice, she would freely point out my mistakes.

Despite these challenges, I remained committed to providing for my family. In 1991, I started selling encyclopedias door-to-door; selling these books became my means of survival. It meant sacrificing personal time and relaxation for the sake of the family.

With numerous responsibilities, enforcing strict discipline at home was difficult. My children could not go out unaccompanied and stayed with my mother when I was away.

Every day was a balancing act, with work demands pulling me one way and family needs tugging me another. It was a constant struggle, trying to find the right balance to give each aspect of my life the attention it deserved. But no matter how tough it got, my family's well-being was always my top priority.

So, I kept pushing forward, facing each challenge head-on, dedicated to providing for and protecting the ones I loved. Every obstacle was just another hurdle to overcome. This was my journey, a testament to my toughness and fortitude.

CHAPTER 7
SELLING SUCCESS

It was heartbreaking for both my parents, especially my father, to see me struggling to make both ends meet. Witnessing his only daughter, a now 21-year-old, in this situation caused him great pain.

Because of my father, my mother had a smooth married life in terms of money. He worked, while my mother enjoyed spending time with friends and sold life insurance as a small side business.

One day, my mother suggested that I try selling insurance. I found the suggestion intriguing. It was something I had not considered before, so I decided to give it a shot. So, my mother introduced me to the insurance industry, and I began selling insurance, too. That was how I got into the insurance business.

At the same time, I started selling Tupperware—surprisingly I became a top seller. I never realized I had a knack for sales. This experience proved invaluable to me in the future.

In 1984, before I became pregnant with my daughter, I was a dancer on television. I participated in competitions and performed with a dance group. Although my time on television was relatively short, lasting only about a year, I poured my energy and focus into it, thoroughly enjoying the experience.

This television experience helped me while I was working in the insurance company. There was a group of elderly ladies who needed help preparing for a company program. They were in need of a choreographer, so they hired me to teach them how to dance. I remember the song I used was *'I am Every Woman,'* and their dancing was the heart of the program.

I excelled in selling life insurance and pension plans. Anything I could sell to make money, I did. I sold Avon, Playtex, Tupperware, and anything else that came my way. My focus was on earning money, and I pursued every opportunity I could, all to help my family.

Yet, selling without a stable income was challenging, especially while my husband could only find work as a sidecar-boy (driving bicycle) in our neighborhood. Meanwhile, I continued to struggle, feeling unhappy that I could not provide enough money to care for my growing children.

My father silently observed our situation. Then one day, he spoke to my husband and said, "I am going to send you to school to become a Merchant Marine." He offered the support because he did not want his daughter to continue struggling.

As a result, my father sent my husband to school. After the training, which lasted about six months to a year, he successfully completed the necessary tests and obtained his Seaman's Book. My father also assisted my husband in finding employment. Due enlarge part to my father's influence and reputation, he successfully secured a job for Lito in the agency.

My husband would be away for 11 months and then returned for a month. He would then again rely on my father's support to find his next job. Whenever he needed to travel abroad for work, he could not simply apply through an agency on his own. He always required my father's help in securing his next position. This attitude of passively relying on my father for help started bothering me.

This was 1991 and my daughter, Mickie, had turned six and was ready to start Kindergarten. Mico, my son, was four then. My husband adopted my daughter and she officially became his daughter, bearing the same last name as the rest of the family. Along with this decision, we also enrolled her in a private Catholic school to begin her academic journey.

My parent's home had a small apartment at the back, my father suggested that we could live in that rental house. He even told us we would not have to make monthly payments and we could live there as a family.

Despite this, I still desired to contribute to the family financially. Eventually, around 1992, I found a job at Encyclopedia Britannica. I worked there for four years, honing my skills in sales and marketing. This

Chapter 7: Selling Success

allowed me to sharpen my abilities in this all important area, which would come to serve me well in the future.

At my job interview, the manager asked what I would do if given a heavy item to sell without knowing if anyone was interested. Without hesitation, I replied that I would sell it. As long as it was a decent job, even if it was cleaning a toilet, I would accept it so that I could contribute to the family. This confidence in my ability to sell and my determination eventually led to my job at Encyclopedia Britannica. So, I began my journey in sales and marketing.

Joining Encyclopedia Britannica was the beginning of my career. Here, I made lifelong friends, including Ferdie, Sylvia, and Amie. They are exceptionally skilled in sales and often won incentives. This included international trips if certain targets were met.

One of my challenges was not having a car and it presented an enormous challenge for my team of five. We would be dropped off in a subdivision and instructed to canvas the area for two hours before returning. Back then, we did not have tools like Alexa or Google Maps. When we visited clients, we had to rely on maps to find the location of the house. Jeepneys or buses were the only source of transportation that we had.

With heavy leatherbound books in hand, we went from door to door, building rapport and hoping that homeowners will allow and trust us into

Chapter 7: Selling Success

their homes. It was a difficult task, knocking on doors and asking strangers to allow us in and then give them a presentation. Every interaction felt like a negotiation, with each homeowner representing a potential commission that would cover my bills. You see, we did not receive a basic salary, only commission for each sale.

Our manager, TM, who was my mentor at that time, encouraged perseverance, reminding me that for every thousand "no," there was always one "yes" at the end. This specific mindset stuck with me. I refused to let rejections discourage me. To this day, I try to turn every setback into an opportunity.

Selling Encyclopedias was not easy. One strategy involved setting up tables in malls and conducting a raffle to invite potential clients to sit and get a presentation. This strategy was called *'Over the Counter'* and would last for a month. My approach was fixed; I insisted on presenting to couples because decisions about such an important purchase always required both parents to agree.

In my country, where education is highly valued, selling a set of Encyclopedia Britannica that cost approximately between 59,000 to 70,000 pesos (about $1,000 to $1,500) was a big deal. This is clearly a significant investment for a middle-class family. Despite all of these challenges, I continued to sell day in and day out.

Chapter 7: Selling Success

When I was with a client and started presenting my product, I would not sell them. Instead, I would convince clients about the importance and benefits of our product. Representing Encyclopedias were not just for parents; they were their children's future.

During my presentations, I insisted on both, husband and wife being present. I saw them as a down payment because their decision directly impacted my livelihood. My goal was simple: *'I needed to make a daily sale to cover my bills.'* It was difficult, but I survived those challenging times, and I believe that I am the better for it.

It was incredible to see how each of my team members at Brittanica have pursued different paths and found success in life. Ferdie is a very successful businessman with several companies and his strategy led him to own a water and filter company in the Philippines. Amie owns her own shipping company and Sylvia is currently living in Canada as a successful realtor. Our friendship remains strong. I will always be grateful to the Britannica family and my colleagues for teaching me resilience and determination throughout my five years in that organization.

My mother disapproved of my job. She believed it was not suitable for a woman, especially with my husband working abroad. Unlike my father, she was not as open-minded. She expressed concern about me being out alone and returning home later in the evening without my

Chapter 7: Selling Success

husband present. She worried about what others might think, she voiced her concerns about how I would be perceived by friends and neighbors.

My husband's reliance on my father's assistance to find jobs. One day, I confronted him, questioning why he could not apply independently. It seemed to me that he lacked initiative. I suggested he try applying to different departments, too. Despite my attempt to change this, he continued in the same pattern. This made me begin to question the future of our marriage. Despite the years we had spent together his lack of ambition was becoming a dealbreaker.

One day, I shared my thoughts with my mother about a possible separation from my husband. I told her I felt our relationship was stagnant and I suggested he return to his family while our children stayed with me. My mother's reaction was one of anger and disbelief. She jumped to conclusions, assuming I must have a boyfriend and questioned my motives. She failed to comprehend my ambition and the frustration I felt with his lack of ambition. Eventually, my husband and I decided to separate. I continued with my work, and there were times when my ex-husband would help care for the children. This was done by mutual agreement, of course.

One evening, I returned home around 11 pm, only to find my ex-husband in the house. Taken aback, I asked my mother why he was there.

Chapter 7: Selling Success

She responded that she felt pity for him and had invited him back. She did this without consulting me or considering my feelings.

This unilateral decision added to the turmoil and distress in my life. Feeling deeply frustrated and unsupported, I packed my bags and told my mother that I would not stay in the house if she continued making decisions on my behalf. My husband and I had already decided to separate. I needed him to prove that he could manage without my father's help. Consequently, I left the house with my children.

Upon leaving, I realized I did not have the resources to pay for anything, not even a place to stay. Overwhelmed with emotions, I broke down in tears and I reached out to my friend Arlene for help. Thankfully, she came to my rescue and helped me find a small room to stay in during this challenging time. When I moved out, I was working for Encyclopedia Britannica during the day and selling products for Seagram Distillers, specifically their liquor, in the evenings. I was hustling hard, going from club to club selling Absolut Vodka. I actually became one of their top sellers. Despite all this, money remained very tight and I had to find something better.

I kept up this intense schedule, hitting up bars night after night for about a year and a half until I no longer needed to. I proved to my mother and ex-husband that I could support my children while ensuring they attended school regularly. However, this juggling act left me mentally

Chapter 7: Selling Success

and emotionally drained, and it tore my family apart. Even my father seemed to agree with my mother's perspective. This further complicated my situation. He was furious with me for leaving my family and neglecting my own life. My father believed that this was my intention, but of course, it was not. I was aware of my actions, and once I had made the decision, there was no turning back.

CHAPTER 8
FROM DREAMS TO DEPARTURE

Around 1994-95, my life took a difficult turn. I was still working two jobs but had left my family. Seeing my kids every weekend became a struggle because my mother was very angry with me. My ex-husband, Lito, was happy because he had my mom on his side. I was out of the house, and he was living there, making it impossible for me to see my children without seeing him. They were punishing me for leaving, and they did not understand that I could not live with my ex-husband anymore. My mother believed that when God puts you together, no one can separate you. But I saw no future with this man. I was ambitious, and he had no ambition. I had to do what I thought was right for me and my family. So, I kept working, even though my mother tried to turn my children against me. My son was only eight years old, and my daughter Mickie was ten.

In 1995, my son, Mico had a terrible accident. He was crossing the street with my family, holding candy. About six or seven people were crossing, and my sister-in-law was holding his hand. Miko dropped his candy, pulled away from his aunt and ran back to get it. A car was coming, but luckily, the driver was very old and driving slowly at about 30 kph. Miko got hit and was dragged under the car. His leg got caught under the

Chapter 8: From Dreams to Departure

tire, and he was severely injured. They took him to the emergency room and called me.

When I got there, I could tell Miko was in a lot of agony. His leg had no skin from the ankle to a bit above where a sock would cover. The nurses were cleaning his wound with a face towel, and he was screaming for me to stop them. They asked if I wanted to do a skin graft. They explained that they would take skin from his thigh to cover the wound. I had no idea what this was. I was confused and scared, and my son was crying. I did not want to cause him more pain. In the end, I decided not to do the skin graft.

At that time, my parents once again tried to make me come back home. Lito also wanted me back in the house. I tried to explain I did not want to come back and that I was doing fine living on my own. We fought a lot over this. I remember Christmas of 1995. I had planned to see my children, but Lito tricked me. He said we were going somewhere else, but the taxi took us back to the house. Again, I explained that I did not want to go back.

When we got to the house, we had another fight. Everyone was there at the house: Lito, my parents, and my children. Lito dragged me upstairs and forced me to stay. He pushed me onto the bed and put his right hand on my neck, choking me.

Chapter 8: From Dreams to Departure

He threatened to hurt me, and I was terrified. The house was in chaos, with everyone screaming and the children crying. To calm the situation and for my safety, I agreed to stay. I stayed for about a week, but I was miserable. During that week, I did not go to work because my mother accused me of working as a prostitute. Instead of protecting me, she imagined the worst of me and did not trust me. The house was quiet but loveless. There was no happiness in that house, and I felt trapped. I knew I had to leave and find a better life for myself and my children.

Unlike in the United States, in the Philippines, if you say no to your husband, partner, or boyfriend for sex, they usually respect that. But Lito was different. He told me it was my responsibility as a wife to keep him happy. He forced me into a miserable relationship. There was no connection between us. I gave in to his demands because I was afraid and I had no choice.

Afterward, I would just turn away, feeling horrible. Our relationship was awful. I felt trapped and everyone was against me. My children often saw me crying. They were confused and hurt by what was happening. They were also brainwashed by my mother. She believed that a Filipina wife must always obey her husband. Our culture is very religious, and at that time, it was unacceptable for a woman to leave her husband.

My family could not accept that I was an independent and ambitious woman. All I wanted was a better future for me and my children.

Chapter 8: From Dreams to Departure

I knew I could not continue living like this. I told Lito and my mother that I was leaving again after just a week. My mother did not like it, but she could not force me to stay. When my family saw Lito hurting me, especially my younger brother, they became very upset. They wanted to protect me because they saw how much I was suffering. I stood firm in my decision to leave and moved out of the house for good.

By 1996, despite working two or three jobs, I could not provide a good life for my children. So, I decided to go abroad for better opportunities.

In 1996, I went for an interview to become a telephone operator in Dubai at a Pakistani hotel called Avari Hotel. When I decided to leave the country, I did not ask my mother's permission; I simply informed her of my decision to go, knowing she was not happy about it. My father was also not thrilled with the idea of me moving to a foreign country. He had traveled to many countries and had seen the women at the ports selling perfume or other goods but often working as prostitutes. He warned me against tarnishing our family's name. He even said, "If you destroy my name, I will kill you." His harsh words did not scare me. I knew I needed to change my life.

Upon arriving in Dubai, I saw the city as a big chunk of gold, full of opportunities. I vowed to myself that I would no longer work as a salesperson, having had enough of commission-only jobs back in the

Chapter 8: From Dreams to Departure

Philippines. I started as a telephone operator at the Avari Hotel. The hotel was new, located at the Clock Tower in Dubai. During the orientation, they trained us on hotel operations.

In 1996, Dubai was very different from today, with very few buildings. The tallest buildings were the Emirates Towers and the World Trade Center on Sheikh Zayed Road. I worked diligently as a telephone operator. Within a month, the general manager (GM) and front office manager noticed my skills. They saw how well I spoke over the phone and my excellent English.

In the Avari Hotel, most of the staff were Pakistani, Bangladeshi, Indian, and Filipino. After working there for a month as a telephone operator, the front office manager was so impressed that he promoted me to a receptionist position. The promotion was in name only and did not come with a raise, so unfortunately, my salary remained the same. During that time, contracts for jobs like mine included company-provided food, housing, and transportation. The hotel was located in Deira, Dubai, but our accommodation was in Sharjah, which was an hour away. The company was responsible for us, so we were not allowed to live outside the provided accommodation. Meals were available in the hotel's cafeteria, not in the main restaurant.

We had four shifts. One shift started at 3 PM and ended at midnight, called the "graveyard shift." Another shift ran from 11 PM to 8 AM. The

Chapter 8: From Dreams to Departure

shifts rotated, so sometimes I worked in the morning and sometimes in the evening.

Staff could not take taxis to and from work; we had to use the company bus. This bus ride included staff from various countries, all grouped according to their shift schedules. For me, it was my first time meeting people from Pakistan, India, and Bangladesh. The bus was packed with Filipinos, Russians, and Kenyans. I always wore perfume, had a clean uniform, and I always took a shower before work.

However, the smell inside the bus was unbearable. On my first ride, I even vomited because of the strong odors. The next day, I told my front office manager that I could not take the bus anymore. Even though I had no money for taxis, I was determined to find another way. My manager was surprised and asked why. I suggested he should try taking the bus himself. When he did, he realized how bad it was and implemented a rule requiring all staff to shower before getting on the bus.

This made me quite popular among several of my colleagues. Some appreciated the change, while others resented me for speaking up. Regardless, I continued to focus on my work and adapting to my new life in Dubai.

Around this time, I also started making new friends; they came from many different countries. It was fascinating to learn about their cultures and backgrounds. I became particularly close with a group of Filipinas

Chapter 8: From Dreams to Departure

who worked in the same hotel as me. We would often meet up after our shifts to share stories and support each other through the challenges of living abroad. These friendships were a lifeline for me, providing a sense of community and belonging in a foreign land. We continue to keep in touch to this day.

Despite the support from my friends, I still missed my children terribly. I called them whenever I could, but it was not the same as being there in person. Hearing their voices made me both happy and sad. Happy because I could connect with them, but sad because I was not there to see them as they grew. As a mother, it was heartbreaking not being able to see my children grow. I missed their birthdays, holidays, and every life-changing event. No amount of phone calls can make up for this and young children do not understand why; they only know that you are absent.

My mother continued to make it difficult for me to speak with them, often limiting our conversations or making it clear that she did not approve of my decision to leave. But I held on to the hope that one day, I would be able to bring my children to live with me in Dubai or provide them with a better life back in the Philippines.

As the months went by, I became more proficient in my job. I learned how to handle demanding customers, manage the hotel's booking system, and I even picked up a few phrases in Arabic. My confidence grew, and I started to think about my future career prospects. I knew that I did not

Chapter 8: From Dreams to Departure

want to remain a receptionist forever. I had bigger dreams and ambitions, and I was determined to achieve them. Eventually, I was promoted to receptionist.

By that time, I was confident in my ability to connect with people. I did not just sell services; I convinced people by talking nicely to them. The hotel had guests from all over the world, including Russians, Italians, and Germans. Many of them did not speak English well, and when they did, they would speak very slowly. I made sure to talk to them slowly, never making them feel less because of their language skills. Communication was the key, whether it was through body language, hand gestures, or simple words. The guests appreciated my efforts, and many preferred to deal with me directly.

I remember one guest who would not accept his key from anyone but me. This kind of dedication and personal connection made me proud of my work. I always aimed for perfection and never settled for less. I was very determined and focused on my goals in Dubai, like a horse with blinders. I intended to reach my career destination.

After about six or eight months in this role, I noticed two Filipina girls coming into the hotel and heading straight to the sales and marketing office. Curious, I asked my manager who they were. He told me they were sales executives responsible for bringing business to the hotel. Intrigued, I asked how I could become a sales executive. My manager dismissed my

Chapter 8: From Dreams to Departure

interest, saying there were no openings and that it would take two or three years before I could even think about moving to that position. But I did not believe him.

A year into my contract, I learned about the strict rules in Dubai: if you did not finish your two-year contract, you would be sent back home with a ban preventing you from working there again. I did not want to risk that, but I was also restless, looking to get ahead.

I had a client who offered me a job at another company. However, moving to a different company was complicated because the hotel held my passport, which was legal in Dubai at the time.

It prevented staff from leaving the country before their contract was finished. Our front office manager told me that if I wanted to leave, I would need to do something significant for the hotel.

They had a guest who was very angry, and I was tasked with calming him down. Typically, this would be a salesperson's responsibility. I do not remember all the details, but the guest had many complaints. With my interpersonal skills, I managed to turn his anger into satisfaction. I made him feel heard and offered solutions that appeased him.

Despite my efforts, the management did not keep their promise to help me transition to a sales role. I could not take it anymore and decided to leave. When I told them I was moving on, they refused to release my

Chapter 8: From Dreams to Departure

passport. Determined, I went to the GM, Mr. Forsyt, a kind British man. I explained the situation to him, and he released my passport. I then started working as an executive secretary for a Turkish company owned by one of the hotel's regular guests.

However, I quickly found out that the company could not provide me with an employment visa because it was not big enough. Working without a visa in Dubai was risky, and I was worried about my future. Despite the challenges, I remained determined to find a stable, well-paying job that would allow me to support my children and secure our future.

It was now 1997, and I was still searching for a new position. Since I was no longer working at the Avari Hotel, I had moved out of their accommodation and rented my own place. Even though I had told everyone in the Philippines that I would not go back to a sales job, there was a major opportunity for a sales executive that caught my attention.

It was time for me to continue my journey, and this new opportunity led me to Oman.

CHAPTER 9
A NEW BEGINNING IN OMAN

I went for the interview, and it was a German lady who conducted it. She was a bit older than me, maybe three or five years. She was the Director of Sales and Marketing at Sheraton. During the interview, she asked me about my sales experience. I was honest and said I had no experience in the hotel industry. She had a proposal for me. She had just been promoted to Director of Sales and Marketing at Sheraton Oman. She needed someone to support her in her new role, so she asked me if I was willing to go with her and assist her in her new position; without hesitation, I said yes!

When I arrived at Sheraton Oman and had settled in, I met the team. There were already five salespeople working there. The team included an Indian woman, a Filipina, a French lady, a Jordanian, and a German. I was the newest addition to the group, brought in by my boss from Dubai.

On my first day, they gave me a small table and a stack of files. These files were called "dead files," which meant they were for companies that had not done recent business with Sheraton despite efforts to win them over. It was a challenging start for me, especially since I was new to the hotel industry and unsure of what to do.

Chapter 9: A New Beginning In Oman

As a sales executive in the hotel industry, our main responsibility was to bring in guests who would stay at the hotel. Sheraton Oman had around 400 rooms and was owned by the Sheikh of Oman. The GM at the time was German. He entrusted me with the task of turning those "dead files" into business opportunities.

It was a daunting task, but I was determined to learn and succeed. My lack of experience did not hold me back—I was ready to prove myself and hopefully make a name for myself in the hotel industry.

Rose, the sales secretary, was lovely and supportive. She helped me get started and suggested I try telemarketing. Telemarketing meant calling potential clients before visiting them in person. In the hotel industry, clients fall into different categories: corporate clients (big companies such as Microsoft), travel agencies (this was before Expedia existed), and exhibition organizers. My job was to focus on corporate clients.

Since I did not have a driving license yet, I could not visit clients in person, so telemarketing was a good way to start. The GM told me, however, that I would need to get my license. So, I started the process of taking driving tests. Meanwhile, I worked on the "dead files," calling corporate clients and arranging the meetings. I was eager to start making sales calls in person, so I decided to take a taxi to my appointments.

Chapter 9: A New Beginning In Oman

One day, I needed to visit a Jordanian company at the shipping port. I took a taxi, and the driver was wearing a long dress called an abaya, which is common in Oman. As we drove, I noticed the driver kept looking at me in the rearview mirror. Then, I saw his hand moving in a strange way, and I realized he was masturbating. I was terrified. I pretended to call the police on my phone and demanded that he stop the car. He pulled over, and I quickly got out and told him I was calling the police. The taxi sped away and I was left alone and scared, so I called the hotel's bell desk in tears. They connected me to the GM, who asked what happened. I explained that I had been harassed and told him my location. He instructed me to find a safe place, and soon a driver came to pick me up and take me back to the hotel.

Despite this horrifying experience, I did not let it stop me from doing my job. I knew I had to get my driving license as soon as possible. This incident was one of the worst experiences I ever had in the Middle East, but it did not break my spirit. I was determined to succeed, no matter the challenges I faced.

I had been working at the Sheraton for almost a year when I met a special client, Mr. Ali. He was around 60 years old and a significant person in Oman. He was the head of the Ministry of Information. Mr. Ali frequently visited our hotel, always asking for me when he arrived. He would sit in the lobby coffee shop and drink a cup of tea. There, he would chat with me for about 15 minutes almost every day.

Chapter 9: A New Beginning In Oman

Mr. Ali usually gave his business to the Intercontinental Hotel, but one day, he told me about a big event coming to Oman where many international journalists would be attending. He decided to give his business to me instead of Intercontinental. This was a huge opportunity because it involved 120 rooms for three nights, with all expenses covered by the Ministry of Information, including room service, laundry, and minibar. This was a significant business deal, and it made me standout at the Sheraton.

I became known for my hard work and dedication. Every morning, I would be in the office by seven o'clock, an hour before our morning briefing. I spent my days hosting guests, often up to six at a time. The Sheraton had 13 restaurants, including seafood, Italian, and Asian, and I would invite clients to dine with me, sometimes bringing their families. My goal was to build a strong relationship with them, not just to secure immediate business but, more importantly, to establish a long-term rapport.

It was not uncommon for me to entertain a guest late into the night. The GM saw me in the lobby and asked Ali, our front office manager, how I managed to keep up my energy. It did not matter to me whether clients gave me business right away because I did not work for commission, so there was no pressure to meet targets. I had a salary, and my focus was on doing my best in everything I did.

Chapter 9: A New Beginning In Oman

This dedication paid off when Mr. Ali transferred his business from the Intercontinental to the Sheraton. This large booking helped us significantly, and it showed the importance of building good relationships and being persistent in providing excellent service. Despite the challenges and even dangerous situations I faced, like the scary encounter with the taxi driver, I remained determined and focused on my work. This experience in Oman, though it had its challenging moments, also brought valuable lessons and opportunities for personal growth.

In Oman, I shared my apartment with a female colleague who was on my team. We were both sales executives, and although our roles were similar to others, our living arrangements were different. Instead of staying in shared accommodation, we lived in a more comfortable apartment-style setting. We each had our own bedroom with a bathroom, a shared kitchen, and a living room.

I did not consider myself particularly beautiful, but I found myself courted by several men. One of them was a 52-year-old British client who was quite persistent. I was only 30 at the time, so he was much older than me. I was not looking for a boyfriend or intending to get married. My focus was solely on earning money to support my children and ensure they received a good education at a Catholic school back in Philippines.

I tried to make this very clear to him. Despite this, every day, without fail, I would receive a bouquet of flowers from him. They were beautiful,

Chapter 9: A New Beginning In Oman

long-stemmed roses. It was the first time I had ever seen champagne-colored roses. Not knowing what to do with all these flowers, I would share them with Rose, the very nice sales secretary, and my friends Mia and June.

Mia worked in the VIP lounge, and June was the Executive Secretary of the GM. We were all single and often spent time together during and after work.

In addition to the flowers, I also received a lot of snacks. There was a Bahraini man who owned a peanut store and he would frequently send large baskets of peanuts to the hotel. The bell desk would deliver these to me, but I never kept them for myself. Instead, I would give them away, which made me quite popular at the hotel.

One day, my friend from the Philippines called me, crying. She had moved to Dubai but felt lost and scared. She was like a sister to me. We had applied for jobs together in 1996, but her father did not let her go because she was only 19. I reassured her and arranged for her to visit me in Oman for 10 days. The only TV in our flat was in the living room, and it belonged to my colleague, who shared the apartment with me. One day, when my friend was alone, she watched TV to relax and feel closer to home. Later, we went out shopping. When we returned, we saw the TV covered with a towel, which meant we were not allowed to use it. Instead

Chapter 9: A New Beginning In Oman

of confronting my flat-mate, I bought a TV for my bedroom so she could continue to watch without any issues.

The following day, I went to the GM's office and demanded to be moved to another villa because I was unhappy with my living situation. He transferred me later that same day.

Around this time, I was already considering leaving Oman. My friend June found a job in Bahrain and called me, saying they were looking for a guest service manager. I told her I did not know how to handle that role since I was a salesperson, but she believed in me and encouraged me to come to Bahrain.

June, who was the executive secretary of the GM at a hotel called Le Meridien, a lovely resort owned by the Sheikh of Bahrain. She gave my CV to the GM there. They were looking for a Guest Services Manager, which was a new position they were creating. This job combined tasks from different departments, like housekeeping, room service, and bell service into one.

There was already a woman acting as a guest relations manager who knew the job well. She had a team consisting of Moroccan, Filipina, Indian, and Sri Lankan, about 15 people in total. Despite just moving to a new villa in Oman, I decided to apply for the job in Bahrain. I took a week off and went to Bahrain for the interview.

Chapter 9: A New Beginning In Oman

The interview was intense, with a panel of seven people, including the GM, Financial Manager, Front Office Manager, and Human Resources. They asked me many questions for almost two hours. Eventually, I looked at my watch and told them, "You have my number. If you think I am fit for this job, call me. I have a plane to catch." Everyone was surprised, but they understood.

Luckily, I got the job. Now, I had to transfer to Bahrain, so I went to my GM in Oman and resigned. Even though he had just made changes to make me happy, I said I needed to move on. I believe there was nothing they could do to stop me.

I had a month to prepare for my move. I packed my things and finally headed to the airport. It was around 7:30 in the evening. While waiting to board, two immigration officers in green uniforms approached me. They asked if I was 'Imee,' to which I replied yes. They informed me that I would not be allowed to leave the country. I was confused and scared and asked why, but they would not explain. They retrieved my luggage from the plane and handed it back to me. I stood there, bewildered, not knowing what I had done wrong.

I kept calling the GM, but he did not pick up the phone. I called Ali, but nobody was replying. Finally, the PR officer at the airport came to my rescue. During all of this, I felt lost, wondering what I should do next. The PR officer asked for my passport and took it, and then we headed

Chapter 9: A New Beginning In Oman

back to the hotel. It was around 8:30 PM by then. I was scared and asked Ali what was going on. He looked worried and said he did not know why I could not leave the country. I tried calling the GM again, but no answer. Then, I saw him entertaining a client in the hotel's restaurant.

He saw the phone ringing but ignored it. It was clear he wanted to punish me for leaving. I went to Human Resources, but nobody wanted to tell me what was happening. I could not understand how they could hold me back. Ali gave me a room and helped me with my luggage. I could not sleep, worried about what would happen next.

The next morning, at nine o'clock, there was a knock on my door. It was the PR officer, he handed me my passport and told me I was cleared to leave.

They took me to the airport, changed my flight, and I was on my way again. I recall sitting on the plane, praying for it to take off. As I sat there, an immigration officer walked down the aisle towards me. My heart raced; fortunately, he walked past me to talk with someone else. The trauma of that moment was intense. Finally, when the plane took off, I could feel the relief washed over me.

Life in the Middle East was not easy or smooth, but I survived. I took every challenge as a part of my journey to success. I never saw myself as a failure, no matter what went wrong. I fought and showed everyone that no one could break me. This made me stronger and more resilient. I have

Chapter 9: A New Beginning In Oman

a powerful personality, and I am fearless. No one can tell me what I can or cannot do. For me, I will always find a way to make things right. This is who I am.

CHAPTER 10
RISING TIDES OF REAWAKENING

When I reached Bahrain, I was still shaken from my experience at the airport in Oman. My mind was stuck in that frightening scenario, making it hard for me to focus. Despite this, I had to meet with the human resources manager. They needed to get me settled into my new accommodation, open a bank account, and explain my job. It was a lot to take in all at once. I had to absorb everything quickly because there was no time to rest. The very next day, I had to start work.

My new job was at the Le Méridien Hotel in Bahrain, a huge resort with two buildings. One building housed the hotel itself, and the other had recreational facilities like a gym, spa, and other amenities. To get around, people often used a golf cart because the walk was so long. The GM gave me an in-depth job description. My main task was to handle all problems, no matter what they were—electrical issues, engineering problems, or guest complaints. I was informed that if any problem reached the GM's office, I would be fired. This was the level of responsibilities and pressure I had to deal with.

Being an Asian woman, my salary was about 50% less compared to European people, which was part of the reason they hired me. They gave

Chapter 10: Whirlwind Connections

me the most challenging job, though. My office was at a desk near the reception area of the hotel. In the past, this would have been called a guest service desk, where guests would come with their problems or questions. Nowadays, most hotels use counters or even iPads for such interactions, but back then, it was my desk.

I started my first day at six in the morning, trying to put the previous day's events out of my mind. I needed to focus on my new job and get past everything that had transpired in Oman. My job was crucial, and I could not afford any distractions.

Living in Bahrain was a new experience. I had a team of 15 staff members. Among them were three or four Moroccans, five Filipinos, and several butlers who were Indian, Sri Lankan, and Bangladeshi. The butlers had a specific role—they catered to VIP guests. These VIPs did not check in at the reception. Instead, they went straight to their rooms and I often checked them in personally. They had their own private entrance with their VIP elevator.

Despite the challenges and the initial chaos, I adapted to my new role. The job was demanding, but I was determined to succeed. Each day brought new challenges but I faced them head-on, proving my worth and dedication in a demanding job. This experience was a significant step in my journey, showing my resilience and ability to adapt to new and difficult challenges.

Chapter 10: Whirlwind Connections

One notable moment was when a very important person visited the resort. Handling such high-profile guests was part of my job, and it highlighted the level of service we had to provide. Even though I did not personally escort the guest to their room, my role was to ensure everything was perfect before they arrived. This meant thoroughly inspecting the room to ensure it met the highest standards.

As a guest service manager, a position I was new to, I took my responsibilities very seriously. Before any VIP guest's arrival, I made it a point to check every detail in their room. I inspected the curtains meticulously, making sure the blackout curtain and the sheer curtain were perfectly aligned and free of wrinkles. If I found the sheer curtain crumpled, I would ask the housekeeper to replace it immediately.

I worked closely with the executive housekeeper, not just the regular chambermaids. They knew my rigorous standards and would often have the housekeepers ready with a steamer to fix any imperfections I might find. I did not settle for anything less than perfection, and my attention to detail made me unpopular with some of the staff. They found my standards too high and my demands excessive. To me, however, I was determined to excel in my new role.

One of my tasks was to prepare a welcome basket for the VIP guests. This was not just any basket; it included champagne, a variety of Belgian chocolates arranged in three tiers, and a welcome cake. I ensured that the

Chapter 10: Whirlwind Connections

fruit basket contained only the freshest fruits, with no bruised or overripe items. Everything had to be perfect to make the guests feel special and welcome.

The mini-bar in the VIP rooms also came under my scrutiny. I checked every glass, coffee machine, and other amenities for cleanliness. I would hold the glasses by the bottom and lift them to check for fingerprints or smudges. If I found any, I would set the glass aside and call room service to replace it immediately in my presence. This process ensured that everything in the room was spotless and up to the highest standards.

My precise approach was not just about meeting the hotel's standards but to exceed them. I wanted to prove to myself and others that I was capable of excelling in this role. Despite my brief orientation, I aimed to meet the highest of expectations. My competition was myself, and I pushed hard to demonstrate that I could handle my job efficiently and effectively. The job was challenging, and the workload was heavy. Every detail mattered, and I left no room for mistakes. The stress and pressure were immense, but I thrived under these conditions. My goal was not only to avoid embarrassment but also to set the very highest standards for myself and my work. The satisfaction of knowing I had done my job well was my primary motivation.

Chapter 10: Whirlwind Connections

One day, the Princess of Malaysia was checking into our hotel. Whenever she visited Bahrain, she occupied the entire sixth floor, which included presidential suites, junior suites, and connecting rooms. This floor was split into two wings, and it was a big task to manage. The Princess traveled with a large entourage, including maids and a hairstylist, all of whom had their own rooms. When I checked her in, I dealt with her staff. I would never actually see her.

The wealthy people in the Middle East and Asia often paid with cash instead of credit cards. They would prepay for everything, including laundry, meals, and other services. The cash tips were substantial, and I had to split them among my 15 staff members, including the butlers who served the VIP suites.

The butlers provided high-level service, attending to every need of the guests. They shined shoes, handled laundry, ironed clothes, and performed other tasks. Despite the generous tips and the high-profile nature of the job, my staff, especially the Filipinos and Moroccans, were not happy with me. The Filipinas were unhappy because they felt I had taken a position they deserved. The Moroccans, who spoke Arabic and French, did not respect me or follow my instructions. This made my job as a Guest Services Manager very difficult, to say the least.

I often ended up doing tasks myself if they were not done to my standard. I felt a strong responsibility that my department did its very best.

Chapter 10: Whirlwind Connections

This added significantly to my workload and my stress level. My day started early. I was at the cafeteria by 6:00 AM for breakfast and at my desk by 6:30 AM, ready to open everything up for the day. The area where I sat had a long counter for the receptionists, as we handled many tourists, corporate clients, and other guests daily.

Behind me, we had various office equipment, including a fax machine, as our department doubled at the business center. One morning, around 7:30 or 8:00 AM, a German couple staying at the hotel approached me. They were well-known among the staff for their constant complaints. The woman, in particular, complained about everything from noise to the smell of her room and the air conditioning.

On this particular day, she was extremely upset and complained about the noise of the frogs outside. She approached me angrily, ready to vent her frustrations. Despite my own stress and the challenging environment, I remained calm and professional, handling her complaints as part of my job.

I asked the woman to sit down with her husband before addressing her complaints. I complimented her to ease the tension and asked about the noise she mentioned. She explained she had opened the window, which was a mistake since the windows were designed to be soundproof. I reassured her that I would check the window and the AC. She also complained about a strange smell on her pillow. In front of her, I called

Chapter 10: Whirlwind Connections

the housekeeping staff and asked them to change the pillows immediately. They were on their way to the tennis court, so I tried to keep the conversation light and positive. I even told her I would come and watch them play tennis.

This was back in 1998 when cell phones were bulky and pagers were still common. I carried a radio, a large cell phone, and a pager. My job required constant communication, so I always had these devices on me. I notified my colleagues that I would be away from my desk and headed to the tennis court in a golf cart.

At the tennis court, I watched the couple play and clapped my hands to show support. This simple act transformed their attitude toward me. Over the next few days, they stopped complaining and became friendly. I even sent them a 2-tier basket of chocolates, which they greatly appreciated.

My GM was keeping an eye on how I handled my job. The front office manager, however, did not like me. He preferred the German woman who applied but did not get the job. I needed to build good rapport with other department managers, but most doubted my abilities, waiting for me to fail.

Despite the challenges and doubts, I ensured no problems reached the GM's office. I remember one British couple who were celebrating their wedding anniversary. Even though they were not VIPs, I treated

Chapter 10: Whirlwind Connections

them as one. I sent them champagne, flowers, and a cake with an anniversary greeting card. They were surprised and touched, as they had not informed anyone about their special day. The woman was nearly in tears, grateful for the gesture, and they sent me a heartfelt card when they checked out. These small acts earned me numerous compliments from guests, which the GM noticed. Every day, I woke up early, prepared myself for the day, and was in the staff cafeteria by 6:00 AM sharp.

One morning, while I was getting ready, I could not help but reflect on how much had changed since I started this job. My meticulous attention to detail, although not appreciated by everyone, made a significant difference in the guests' experiences. I continued to face challenges from colleagues, but the positive feedback from guests reassured me that I was on the right path.

Despite the adversity, I remained focused on my duties. Each day, I tackled new problems, ensuring every guest felt valued and respected. Whether it was a minor issue or a significant complaint, I handled everything with the same level of care and professionalism. Over time, my efforts began to pay off. Slowly but surely, some colleagues started to see the value in my approach. The initially skeptical staff began to realize that my high standards were not about making their lives difficult but about maintaining the hotel's reputation and ensuring guest satisfaction.

Chapter 10: Whirlwind Connections

As I continued to build a rapport with the guests and some of my colleagues, I noticed a shift in the atmosphere. The hotel staff started to work more cohesively, understanding that our primary goal was to provide the best possible experience for our guests. My relationship with the housekeeping team improved significantly. They began to appreciate my thorough inspections, understanding that it was a crucial part of maintaining the hotel's standards. My dedication to my role did not go unnoticed. Guests frequently expressed their gratitude and word of mouth about the exceptional service at the hotel spread. The GM's trust in my abilities grew, and he became more supportive of my efforts.

My friends, Mia and June, were working in the same hotel. They were the ones who helped me get the job. Mia worked in sales and marketing, and June was the executive assistant to the GM. One day, after about a week, Mia called me over.

"I need you to come here," she said.

"I can not leave my desk," I replied.

So, she came to me, holding a brochure. It was a three-fold brochure of the hotel featuring a picture of a British guy holding a tennis racket and playing with a lady.

"This guy, Ric is the assistant manager of the recreation department," Mia said. "Ric is single. He is tall and a really nice guy."

Chapter 10: Whirlwind Connections

"But he is not here; he is on vacation," she added.

"So what?" I responded. "I am not looking for a boyfriend."

Mia thought I was lonely and sad, but I was focused on my career. Since leaving the Philippines, I had not thought about getting a boyfriend. I was ambitious and career-oriented, and I did not want any distractions or complications.

Three weeks later, I went to the cafeteria at six o'clock in the morning, as usual. I was always alone. I got my coffee but did not eat breakfast since it was not available until 6:30 or 7:00. I saw a guy having coffee on the other side of the table. It was Ric. He was also an early riser and a workaholic. We did not look at each other.

Every day, we met in the cafeteria at the same time but never talked. One day, Ric looked at me and smiled. I smiled back. I did not know it then, but he had been asking around about me. When he returned from vacation, he found out that I was the guest service manager. Le Méridien had around 300 staff members, so it was impossible to know everyone. Ric was especially disadvantaged because he worked in a different building.

Ric sent one of his staff to give me a small, one-sheet, A4-size paper. On it, there was a drawing of a skeleton holding a key and a heart. I did

Chapter 10: Whirlwind Connections

not understand it at first. Then, I read the note that said, "You are holding the key to my heart."

I thought, "Okay... that is weird." I was not easily impressed by such things. I had always been aloof, making it clear to men that they had to prove themselves worthy of my time and attention. I was not the kind of woman who fell for sweet gestures easily. My focus was always on my career, my goals and my children.

I did not pay much attention to Ric's attempts to impress me, but he kept trying. What I did not know was that he already had a girlfriend, another Filipina. Despite this, he kept chasing me. One time, I went to the spa next to the recreation area where Ric worked. He approached me and asked if I was okay. I told him I was there to visit the travel agency at the front of the spa. It was here that I met my soon to be friend Lisa who worked there. That was the first time I met her, and she would later become one of my best friends.

As my relationship with Ric started to take off, there was a party that my friend June was invited to. She asked me, Lisa and Mia to go along with her. The party was a Filipino gathering hosted by a friend of Ric's. I went, dressed in fitted red pants and a backless top that showed my belly. I was always confident in my looks and liked to dress in a way that showed off my figure. At the party, Ric flirted with me. I had no idea he had a girlfriend who was at the party as well.

Chapter 10: Whirlwind Connections

As the night went on, I noticed that people were starting to talk about me. My friends told me it was best if we left early, so we did. The next day at work, I received a call. The person on the other end was cursing at me and trying to smear my reputation. She accused me of stealing Ric from her friend. I told her that I had no idea what she was talking about and that I did not deserve to be treated that way. I found out later that Ric and his girlfriend had broken up that night. Over time, we eventually became boyfriend and girlfriend.

I later learned that Ric's girlfriend, Christie, worked in the same hotel. She was very jealous, and their relationship had been a rocky one. Ric told me they broke up because of her jealousy, even though we were not involved at that time. He said he was done with her and focused on me. Unbeknownst to me, their breakup was more complicated. While he claimed they were over, Christie still thought they were together. Eventually, he cut all ties with her completely and started focusing on me instead.

Ric and I continued to grow closer and became a couple. Despite the complications, we managed to navigate our relationship while working in the same hotel. This marked the beginning of a new chapter in my life, one filled with both challenges and unexpected turns.

That was at the end of 1998. Our relationship became serious, and we decided to move in together. I did not leave my place; I just went back

Chapter 10: Whirlwind Connections

and forth. As the relationship grew deeper, issues arose at the hotel. You see, the relationships between staff members were not allowed. Our relationship was secretive by necessity, but many people began to notice, making it hard to hide.

Ric and I lived together in Bahrain for three or four months. To continue our relationship, Ric decided to find another job in Dubai. He was a Recreation Manager's Assistant, and I was the guest service manager. One day, I saw his payslip and discovered that his salary was the same as mine. I was unhappy about this since I had a higher position. I did not say anything, but when Ric found a job in Dubai, I decided to leave my job in Bahrain too. It was not fair that I, in a higher position, earned the same salary as a second-in-command just because he was British.

In March or April 1999, we moved to Dubai. At that time, it was not allowed for an unmarried man and woman to live together in one apartment. If the government or any legal authority found out, they would deport us immediately. Since we loved each other, we decided to get married. We tied the knot in March 1999 in Dubai.

CHAPTER 11
THE SHIFTING SANDS OF LIFE

Ric found a job in Dubai, and that was when we moved there and got married in 1999. He worked at a four-star hotel as a Recreation Manager, no longer an assistant. I worked at Metropolitan Hotel as a sales executive, but he was not happy and saw me as a competition instead of being proud of me. When I got promoted to Sales Manager, he disliked it even more.

In May 1999, we went to England to get married again in the Birmingham Courthouse. I met Ric's family during this visit. After spending one month in England, we return to Dubai.

In late 1999, Ric got a job offer at (The Empire Hotel and Resort), now *The Empire Brunei*. We moved there in January 2000. He worked as the Recreation Resort Manager at a hotel owned by one of the Princes of Brunei and one of the world's wealthiest men. It was at this time that I left the hotel industry in an attempt to keep the peace in our marriage.

Brunei was strict and different from what we were used to. Alcohol was not allowed anywhere, so we had to drive, exit and re-enter Miri,

Chapter 11: The Shifting Sands of Life

Malaysia just to buy alcohol and store it at home. We were not happy in Brunei and stayed only a year.

In 2001, Ric got an offer from the World Trade Center in Dubai, so we returned. We initially lived in Jumeirah before moving to an apartment provided by the World Trade Center. We were at home on September 11, 2001, watching the events unfold in New York. Living in Dubai as an expatriates during that time was tough. We eventually moved into a safer apartment at the World Trade Center.

Around 2003-2004 I started working with Emirates Airline travel department (Arabian Adventures). Despite my career change our relationship continued to be strained. My brother, who came to Dubai for our wedding and decided to stay and work, saw how miserable our life was, with frequent fights and arguments, despite loving him deeply and doing things such as changing my lifestyle and appearance just to please him. His jealousy and distrust of me were a constant source of conflict between us.

Ric and I had many friends in Dubai. We often had girls' and boys' nights out. During one girls' night out, we were at an Irish pub, having fun and dancing. I danced with a gay Filipino friend, swaying our hips. Ric showed up unexpectedly with his friends, he saw us dancing and gave me a bad look in front of everyone. He called me a slut, which left me humiliated, and then walked away. I chased after him, leaving my purse

Chapter 11: The Shifting Sands of Life

behind and begging for his forgiveness. He threw his wedding ring in my face dramatically.

In 2004, for my birthday, I wanted to visit my family in Chicago. Ric bought me a ticket as a present, and I went in September. I stayed for two weeks and then returned. Unknown to me, while I was away, he had been unfaithful. I was blind to his cheating and never suspected anything, as I trusted him completely.

I went to Chicago for a holiday, the first time I had ever visited the United States. I stayed with my cousin and family there. This included my uncle, who has since passed away. I was there for two weeks, and when I returned, I had no idea that Ric had started having an affair. He became involved with one of his staff, a Filipina receptionist. My instincts made me suspicious, but I also wanted to trust him.

One day, I noticed his phone was constantly receiving messages. They were text messages exchanged with another woman. This of course made me very uneasy. I later found out they were planning a rendezvous in the parking lot at the World Trade Center. I followed him, when I saw him meeting up with a Filipina girl, I became furious. I confronted her and started pulling her hair in anger. Ric intervened, physically pulling me away and throwing me to the ground. He told me to go home and that we will talk about it later. I was shocked and humiliated. *How could he choose her over me, his wife?*

Chapter 11: The Shifting Sands of Life

After this, our relationship spiraled downwards. We fought every day, and I was miserable. I could not focus on work. I was constantly worried and suspicious about Ric's infidelity and whereabouts. During a visit to my gynecologist, I found out that my health was not as optimal as I believed it to be; I was not well. The reality and depth of his betrayal began to sink in, but I did not want to believe it. My love for him blinded me to the truth.

In late 2004, Ric asked for a separation. He said he had fallen out of love with me. I was devastated and did not understand what had gone wrong. Despite my love and loyalty, he wanted to leave. He started to make significant decisions without consulting me, like buying a new car, while he only got me a secondhand car, which only crushed my self-esteem even further.

Our relationship had become toxic. We shared a bed but remained distant. My brother, who stayed with us, witnessed the constant screaming and fighting. One day, Ric packed his luggage and announced he was moving out. Desperate, I clung to his leg, begging him not to leave. He walked out, leaving me broken and in tears.

When Ric left me, I was alone in a three-bedroom apartment. My two brothers, Roy and Rad, and my friends had no idea what I was going through. I lost my appetite and became extremely skinny, dropping to a

Chapter 11: The Shifting Sands of Life

24-inch waist and weighing only 110 pounds. I started chain smoking and my friends started calling me "J Lo" because of my appearance.

After Ric left, I became a shadow of myself. At work, I sat at my computer, dealing with complaints and emails, barely eating. My boss noticed my distress and sent me home. I hated going home because it meant being alone. I removed all the pictures of us, and I survived on black coffee and cigarettes. I lost so much weight that I nearly became anorexic, vomiting any food I tried to eat and crying a river of tears.

Every day was the same: crying myself to sleep and waking up crying. I called my mother, only to receive a cold response about what would happen to her without my financial support. She said nothing about how she cared for me or loved me. I reassured her that her allowance would not stop and hung up. Still crying, I called a friend, Mel, in Scotland, who comforted me over the phone for at least half an hour.

In Dubai, the weekend was Friday and Saturday. One Friday, I was alone in my house, exhausted and crying. I felt like I was floating, disconnected from reality. I lay on the couch, and at 3 PM, I experienced an out-of-body sensation. I saw myself lying there, unable to wake up. My son appeared in a dream, calling out to me, and I woke up crying, thinking I had died for a moment.

Nobody knew the depth of my despair and I had no one to confide in or hug. One day, unable to bear it any longer, I drove myself to the

Chapter 11: The Shifting Sands of Life

hospital. I felt like my heart was about to burst. My best friend in Dubai, Lenie was supportive, but even she did not fully grasp the extent of my suffering.

Lenie saw my car parked at Emirates Hospital on Jumeirah Beach Road. She became worried and went inside to find me on an IV drip. I had been admitted with very low blood pressure. I had not eaten for days, and the doctor said I was severely dehydrated and depressed. Lenie, the sweetest person, took me home with her. She had two kids, Kelly, then about 10 years old, and Calvin, around 11. Kelly, now an actress in the Philippines, was already modeling in Dubai. I shared Kelly's room for the next two months.

We would play Mahjong and cards, with two tables set up. I had to keep myself busy because I did not want to go home to that empty apartment. Everyone kept asking me how I got so skinny, and I just told them I drank coffee. For six months, nobody knew that Ric had left me.

In 2005, I told everyone I could not do this anymore and decided to go back to the US. I stayed with my cousin Ron. I had friends across the US, including Las Vegas, New York, and San Francisco. Whenever I visited, I made sure to see them. During this time, the only ones who knew my pain were Ron and May.

One day, Ric called, crying and begging me to come back and told me that he could not live without me. He said he had a new apartment and

Chapter 11: The Shifting Sands of Life

he wanted me to furnish it with him, like a husband and wife. He then sent me a ticket to come back to Dubai. Despite my resolve, I was still in love with him. My cousin May talked to him on the phone, telling him to let me go, but I eventually agreed to return to Dubai.

When I arrived back in September 2005, Ric and I bought appliances and moved into the new apartment. Shortly after, he started acting suspiciously again. One night, he left, saying he needed to think. He did not return until the next morning, making up a flimsy excuse. I checked his car and found two empty meal boxes from McDonald's, confirming my fears.

I tried to talk to him, but he avoided me. The apartment was a mess with boxes everywhere. I was still smoking heavily, crying silently. My elder brother found me in this state and begged me to let Ric go, comparing him to a bird that might return if set free. My brother's words were filled with love and concern. He could see how much pain I was in. He gave me a hug and said if I can only take the pain in your heart, I would.

I called my daughter, who was 19 at the time, seeking comfort. She asked how old I was when I met Ric, and I told her 32 years old. She then said, "Mom, if you could live 32 years without Ric, you can live another 32 years without him." Her words hit me hard, making me realize I

Chapter 11: The Shifting Sands of Life

needed to move on. The next day, as he was getting ready, I told him we needed to talk.

He sat down, and I told him, "Why did you ask me to move in with you again?" He replied without hesitation, "Because I wanted to make sure I did not love you anymore." I felt as if the breath had been knocked out of me. I told him, "I am done. I have no more energy," and begged him to let me go.

The following day, I left everything behind, including my car, and took only one bag. I got into a taxi, crying. The driver asked where I wanted to go, and I said, "Just drive."

It was then I remembered my friend Cindy. She was a German married to a Director of food and beverage at Shangri-La Hotel. They lived in a nice villa in Jumeirah with their two kids. I called Cindy, who also knew Ric and told her I did not know what to do or where to go. She said, "Come to my house," so I asked the taxi driver to take me there.

It was now December 2005, I bought a one-way ticket to New York and was planning to stay with my friend Raquel. My idea was to leave on December 29th. Cindy suggested I stay longer and meet a client looking for an executive assistant. I told her I did not want to work in Dubai anymore, but she insisted I stay. Cindy gave me a room with a princess bed. There I lay, crying my eyes out. Cindy set up an interview for me

Chapter 11: The Shifting Sands of Life

and the president of the company for January 2, 2006. I planned to demand a high salary, expecting he would reject me.

I wore a white suit to the interview, feeling confident and professional. The interviewer was a German-Italian man who spoke little English. He told me he was opening a company in Dubai and needed an executive assistant. When he asked what I wanted, I listed high demands, expecting him to say no. To my surprise, he agreed to everything and told me to start the next day, January 3, 2006. At that moment, my life changed. Suddenly, I went from deep anxiety and depression to becoming a very confident once again, a woman working on my own terms.

On January 6, he told me I needed to go to Switzerland for training. I had never experienced winter in my life. He advised me to buy snow boots, thermal wear, gloves, and other winter gear. He gave me a budget to shop for all the necessary things that I would need. I flew to Switzerland and stayed in a small bed-and-breakfast in Zug, near Luzern. The hotel was across from a big lake, which was entirely frozen over.

The staff in our main office spoke very little English, speaking mostly Swiss German. The executive assistant of the Swiss Branch took care of me. My room was in a separate building and to go to breakfast, I had to bundle up for the winter's cold. I walked outside to get to the breakfast area, which was just bread and cheese. As an Asian, I missed having rice for breakfast. I stayed in Switzerland for almost a month,

Chapter 11: The Shifting Sands of Life

working long hours and never seeing the sun. One day when I was off, I finally saw it and the snow. I went outside, sat by the frozen lake, and let the snowflakes fall on my tongue. It felt surreal, like a scene from a calendar picture.

After returning from Switzerland, my boss told me my job was to find a local sponsor and assist wealthy Germans who wanted to become established in Dubai. At this time, I was still working under my husband's visa, not my boss's, as we had not divorced yet.

In 2006, I worked with affluent Germans, Italians, and Swiss people who wanted to open a branch office from Germany or Switzerland to Dubai. I had a very good relationship in the bank and helped my boss open an account without any complication. We dealt with large sums, and I lived comfortably with a high salary. I did not have my own apartment yet, so I stayed at Lenie's house for a few months.

My boss would come and go to Dubai from Switzerland. We did not have a physical office in Dubai—just my phone. When our clients arrived, my job was to arrange for a local sponsor to enable them to become established in Dubai. This included arranging for resident visas, converting their driving license, as well as opening a bank account and setting up their own offices.

Our company was a trustee company based in Switzerland. In Switzerland, a local person was allowed to have multiple companies in

Chapter 11: The Shifting Sands of Life

their own name. My boss, who had a Napoleon complex (also known as Short-Man Syndrome), was quite an authoritative person who liked to show off. I remember when he bought a brand new sports car using his credit card. He was not very happy with the sound of an overspeed alarm, and he asked me to have it removed from the car. He lived in a condo by the marina, and I managed it for him. He then bought a large villa with four bedrooms, but he still lived in a condo by the marina, which I had furnished.

Meanwhile, I stayed with Lenie and spent my free time at the beach. Ric kept calling me. I found I still had strong feelings for him. He asked me to meet him for coffee, and of course I agreed. He said he knew I still loved him—in a way, it was true—but he did not want me back. He just did not want anyone else to have me; he loved to manipulate me in this way.

One day, out of anger, I bought a new car. This was the very same car that Ric loved and coveted. When he saw me driving it, he immediately asked me out to dinner. He took me to the Japanese restaurant in Emirates Tower. I wore a mini skirt and felt confident.

During dinner, he told me he knew I still loved him. I replied, "This is the last time you are going to see my face. I want my self-esteem and confidence back. You hurt me and broke my heart. You are just a part of my past now, a chapter in my life that I have closed." He said I was

Chapter 11: The Shifting Sands of Life

hurting his feelings, and I told him that the pain he had caused me would scar me for life. But that I would overcome all the pain he had dealt me, that I would rise again.

By 2006, I was beginning to assert myself. I heard Ric had moved to Philippines with a Filipina woman that same year. In 2008, I returned to Manila for a holiday. Ric asked me to meet him in Starbucks. There, he asked me to sign the divorce papers. I agreed and signed on the condition that I could keep his last name.

One day, my boss decided to go to India for business. He was gone for three days. When he returned, he wanted to move into his new villa. The villa was still unfurnished, but as usual, I took on the challenge. In those three days, I managed to move everything from his condo to the new villa. I set up cable TV, internet and hired housekeepers to clean and arrange everything so that the villa would be move-in ready when my boss returned. The only thing missing were the curtains since I did not know his preference.

When my boss called and asked where to go back to, I told him he could move into his villa. He was shocked and could not believe I had moved everything in only three days. Right down to having his clothes in the cupboard.

I was available for my boss 24/7 when he was in Dubai. I did everything for my boss except sleep with him. I handled his laundry, food,

Chapter 11: The Shifting Sands of Life

restaurant bookings, and guests. Whenever he traveled, which was always first or business class, he could have a limousine pickup arranged. But instead, he always preferred to have me pick him up, no matter the hour, because he paid me.

One night, he asked me to take him and three guests to a Lebanese restaurant. I reserved a table and managed everything, but I was tired and had an appointment the next morning. When I told him I needed to leave, he treated me poorly, saying I could not leave until he said I could because he signed my cheque. Fed up, I handed him his car keys and quit right there in front of his clients.

The next morning, he called as if nothing happened, but I reminded him I quit. He threatened to sue me, but I pointed out that my visa was not under his sponsorship, and I had the support of his sponsor, my friend. He could not do anything to me.

At that time, Dubai was already struggling with the global financial crisis. Investors left, and the city became a ghost town. So, I decided it was time to leave. I had already quit the job, and I saw there was nothing else for me there. So, instead of staying there any longer, I decided to return home to Manila.

In February 2010, I returned to the Philippines. I had a condo and a car there and would visit my daughter's house daily to prepare food for my grandkids. The problem was I had no income, only expenses. This

Chapter 11: The Shifting Sands of Life

stressful period was a stark contrast to my previous life, which was traveling between Switzerland and Dubai, always in business class and living independently. This new life that I have chosen was a complete flip to the life I had.

I was home, but I did not know what to do in the Philippines!

CHAPTER 12
STRIVING TO BRIDGE THE DIVIDE

As time went by, I found myself staying in my condominium, which was about an hour away from my daughter's house. Every day, without fail, I would go to her house at six o'clock in the morning to prepare food for my grandkids. That became my routine. Despite my efforts, money was tight, and I found myself increasingly unhappy with the situation.

We attempted to start a small business as a supplier to two local restaurants, but it did not last. A restaurant had placed orders with us but required receipts and invoices. At that time, we could not open a trade license because we were working at home. This situation led to the collapse of our business. We ended up selling to the public in small quantities, but it was barely enough to keep us afloat. My savings were dwindling rapidly, and I fell ill, losing my voice for eight months due to laryngitis, likely caused by the pollution. It had been a long time since I lived in my home country, and I could not tolerate the pollution anymore.

Realizing I needed to make a change, I decided I had to leave. Although I had a visa for England, I did not want to go there. I had few friends and relatives there, and the weather was often rainy and gray.

Chapter 12: Striving to Bridge the Divide

Instead, I thought about going to the United States. I had a tourist visa and it was still good for another five years.

By April 2011, I was struggling to pay the mortgage on my condominium and my car loan. The stress was overwhelming, and I did not know what to do. I made the difficult decision to leave the Philippines and my children once again. This time, I set my sights on the United States. Before I left, I contacted friends and found one in Clearwater, Florida. She was my colleague from Encyclopedia Britannica and offered me a place to stay for a week while I figured out my next steps.

I purchased a round-trip ticket so as to comply with travel regulations and headed to the United States with two large suitcases. I once again left my home in Philippines. When I arrived, my friend helped me find a room to rent for $500 a month. With limited money and no job, I faced a tough situation.

I tried applying for jobs but could not provide a social security number, so I was not hired. With no money to pay for my room, I reached out to other friends. A Polish man who wanted to open a restaurant in Clearwater reached out to me. He offered me $100 a day to help get it ready. Out of necessity, I agreed, even though I had no papers or right to work. I handled everything from dealing with contractors to organizing merchandise. However, he did not pay me after a week of work, leaving me devastated and frustrated.

Chapter 12: Striving to Bridge the Divide

A friend in the Filipino community in Clearwater introduced me to a man who organized Filipino waiters and bartenders for weddings. He asked if I wanted to work as a waiter at an event. Desperate for money, I agreed. I bought black pants, a white shirt, and comfortable shoes. The job was grueling, lasting from two in the afternoon until three in the morning. I had never waited tables before and found the work incredibly hard. I worked for 12 hours, lifting tables and chairs, serving guests, and then cleaning up afterward.

By the end of the night, I was exhausted, and my feet were covered in blisters. Despite the pain, I needed the money and continued to work. Each night, I cried, unsure of what my next step should be. Eventually, I contacted a friend in Las Vegas, hoping for better opportunities.

In Las Vegas, I stayed with my friend, Lisa, who helped me find temporary work. The job market was tough, and I struggled to find something stable. The constant stress and uncertainty took a toll on my health. I was mentally and physically exhausted. Despite all of this, I tried to stay positive and focused on finding a solution.

During this period, I often reflected on my life. I thought about my years as an executive assistant, traveling between Switzerland and Dubai, living a comfortable life. It was a stark contrast to my current situation. I had gone from business class flights and luxury hotels to struggling to make ends meet in a foreign country. The hardest part was being away

Chapter 12: Striving to Bridge the Divide

from my family. I missed my son, daughter and grandkids daily. I felt guilty for not being able to support and provide for them as I had before. This guilt fueled my determination to keep going, to find a way to provide for them again.

So basically, what I was doing in the United States was moving from city to city and state to state. It was 2011, and by April or May, I found myself in Clearwater Beach, specifically Pier 60 which was beautiful. I would go there almost every day, dropped off by a friend who had taken a liking to me. He would drop me off at nine in the morning, and I would spend the day contemplating my future until four o'clock. I felt utterly lost and without options. It was like I was back at the beginning, before I had moved to Dubai.

In my despair, I decided to reach out to my cousin Ron in Chicago. I called him, explaining my situation, and he agreed to let me stay, but he was going to the Philippines soon. My friend, Raquel, helped by sending me a ticket from Florida to Chicago. When I arrived, I stayed with Ron for a few days before he left, and then I moved in with my other cousin, May, who had a two-bedroom apartment. We were the same age and made plans together. I thought things were looking up.

However, cousin May had a boyfriend who stayed over at night and was often there during the day while she was at work. After almost a week, May sent me an email saying her landlord had found out I was

Chapter 12: Striving to Bridge the Divide

staying there, and I had to leave immediately. I begged for a week to figure out my next steps, but she insisted I be gone by the time she got home.

Desperate, I sold one of my Louis Vuitton bags, a limited edition, on Craigslist for about $4,000. We met at the Louis Vuitton store in Westfield Mall in Schaumburg, Illinois, to make the exchange. With the money, I booked a night at La Quinta Inn and spent the night depressed, unsure of what to do or where to go next.

I reached out to other family members, but no one could help. Finally, a friend in Indianapolis invited me to stay. To save money, I took a Greyhound bus with my heavy luggage. It was my first experience with long-distance bus travel in the US, and the Chicago station was full of homeless people pushing carts loaded with their meager possessions.

After I arrived in Indianapolis, I stayed with an older woman, a former friend of my mother, and her much younger boyfriend.

I was desperate to find a way to stay in the US legally, so I asked if the boyfriend would marry me for convenience. They took offense and accused me of flirting with him. Her younger daughter, who knew me from our neighborhood, joined them in demanding I leave immediately. I was shocked by their accusations and conniving behavior.

Chapter 12: Striving to Bridge the Divide

Leaving most of my belongings behind, I called my cousin Ron. He told me to come back to Chicago. I took an Amtrak train, arriving at three in the morning. Ron picked me up and took me back to his place, but I could only stay for a week. I became the babysitter for the granddaughter, but the arrangement was not sustainable.

Each move, each disappointment, felt like a step backward. My life was a far cry from the security and comfort I once knew. The constant stress of finding a place to stay, the lack of money, and the overwhelming feeling of being a burden weighed heavily on me. Yet, I was not willing to give up. I had to find a way to rebuild my life and provide for my family again.

While in Chicago, I continued to look for work. The job market was tough, especially without proper documentation. I reached out to friends and acquaintances, hoping for a lead. My network became my lifeline, and I chased any opportunity, no matter how small.

I was running out of options and I did not know what to do. I called my friend, Lisa from Las Vegas again. She was very friendly and is still one of my best friends today. Feeling lost, I reached out to her. She told me to come over, so I stayed with Lisa for three days. My life in the United States was incredibly hard. By this time, I had overstayed my visa. I had never been in this kind of situation before. I had never been illegal in a country. I thought it would be easy, but it was far from that.

Chapter 12: Striving to Bridge the Divide

I had no plans to get married again. After Ric, I felt that I was not very lucky with men. I always ended up hurting myself or hurting somebody else. I decided that I was not going to marry again unless it was for love, not for convenience. My stay with Lisa did not work out because she only had three bedrooms, which were all occupied. Her mother, father, and son were there, as well as Lisa and her husband. I slept in Lisa's son's room. He was eight or nine years old at the time, which was okay, but it was still tough. After three days, I decided to leave.

I called my friend in New York, Raquel. She could not give me shelter or a job, but she helped by sending me a ticket to wherever I wanted to go. I decided to go to California. In Palm Springs, a friend of Lisa's told me that I could stay there and work as a caregiver. There was an agency that accepted anyone, with or without proper documentation, to be a caregiver. This meant being paid under the table.

Before that, I got an offer in Newport Beach, California, so I went there first. I worked in a nursing home, caring for three patients. I had no prior experience being a caregiver, but despite this, they hired me. One patient had dementia, another was in hospice care, and the third was an older man with a condition that required his food to be in liquid form because he could not chew or swallow properly.

The dementia patient often wet the bed without realizing it. The hospice patient was bedridden and needed a daily bed bath. The elderly

Chapter 12: Striving to Bridge the Divide

man needed to be moved from his bed to a wheelchair, and his food had to be prepared specially. I did all this on my own, with very little sleep, because I was responsible for all three. If something happened to them, I could be in serious trouble.

Every day, I got up at four o'clock to prepare breakfast for the three patients. I bathed the old man and moved him to his wheelchair. I bathed the dementia patient and gave the hospice patient a bed bath. I also cleaned the facility.

One day, I pulled a muscle in my back while lifting the elderly man. I could not move and developed a fever. My fever was very high and I did not know what to do. So I called Lisa once again and told her I could not move. She was furious but also concerned. She sent her cousin, who lived in a nearby town, to pick me up. Lisa could not come herself because Newport Beach was far from her place. Her cousin Nell, drove me to Palm Springs. There, I contacted another agency that accepted people without proper documents.

I filled out my application and waited. One day passed, then two, three, four, almost five days. The house where I stayed was next to a church, so I went there every day. I would pray, feeling almost ready to give up. I was exhausted physically, mentally, and emotionally. I had no money, no house, and worse of all, no prospects.

Chapter 12: Striving to Bridge the Divide

In my desperation, I called a friend who used to be my neighbor in Philippines, who now lived in Texas. Her name is Nida, and she became my angel. Nida was four years older than me and worked as a caregiver while attending nursing school. She had two children, one about eleven years old and the other sixteen or seventeen.

Despite her busy life, she welcomed me to her home in San Antonio, Texas. I bought a one-way ticket from Palm Springs to San Antonio and went to Nida's place. In every house I stayed in, I tried not to be a burden. I helped out with anything I could—taking care of the kids, cleaning, cooking, doing laundry. Nida was the only person who kept me for three months without any complaints. This was great but I still had no legal papers and was getting tired, constantly trying to figure out my next move.

By December 2011, I was in San Antonio. Nida, who was a member of the Church of Christ, did not celebrate Christmas. She did offer me support and shelter. As Christmas approached, I felt myself missing my children more than ever. I felt very low and depressed. I needed to experience Christmas, so I asked Lisa if I could come and visit, as her mother and father were like family to me.

Lisa invited me to come over, so I took a Greyhound bus from San Antonio to Nevada. The bus ride was long, with many stops. On one of the stops, I was seated at the front of the bus, on the right side, with the

Chapter 12: Striving to Bridge the Divide

driver on the left. A young girl who looked to be about 17 or 18 years old sat next to me. We chatted, and people remarked that we looked like mother and daughter. This made me miss my family much more.

At the Amarillo station in Texas, the bus stopped and a man wearing jeans and a white shirt with a badge came on board. He looked like a police officer. He asked me where I was going and why. I told him I was going to Las Vegas to spend Christmas with friends. His questions made me very nervous because I was in the country illegally, having overstayed my visa. He asked to see my passport.

He said, "Where is your passport?"

I did not know but law enforcement officers cannot request documentation, being a free country, and they are not allowed to ask about your status. But in my ignorance, I handed over my passport.

He asked, "Are you two mother and daughter?"

I said no, but he did not ask the girl sitting next to me.

Then he asked, "Where is your luggage?"

I pointed to it, and he ordered me to get it and open it. I did as he asked, feeling all eyes on me as everyone watched in shock. After he looked through my luggage, he simply said, "Okay, close it," handed back my passport, and left.

Chapter 12: Striving to Bridge the Divide

When he left, I was shaking and nervous. I feared he might report me as illegal and that I could be deported. I called Lisa, praying and wondering if I was going to be deported. Lisa told me to stay calm and picked me up at the Boulder station in Nevada. I was still shaken, and the passengers on the bus were upset by how I had been treated. An old lady on the bus even swore, expressing her anger at the man who had interrogated me.

When I reached Lisa, I hugged her, wondering if I was going to be deported. She told me, "You can not go state to state anymore because you are not legal." I knew she was right. I spent Christmas and New Year with Lisa and her family, but afterward, I went back to Texas to stay with Nida.

It was now January, and we were trying to figure out how I could earn a living. I suggested starting a cleaning business together, so Nida got a trade license, and we started a business called "Made in the Philippines." We cleaned houses together, with me usually handling the bathrooms and the upstairs if it was a two-story house, while Nida cleaned downstairs. All the while, she was holding down a regular job, as well as studying to be a nurse. I admired her determination and hard work.

My job was to find clients, so I made flyers and did everything I could to get us work. We managed to get some clients, but it still was not enough for me. Without papers, I could not find a stable job, and after

Chapter 12: Striving to Bridge the Divide

two months, I was feeling down again. By March, I decided I could not continue like this and told Nida I was going back to the Philippines. Nida was not happy with my decision. She screamed at me, saying, "You can not do this. You have already spent so much time here. If you go back, you will never return to the US because you are overstaying."

I was at a loss, not knowing what to do. In frustration, she suggested, "Why don't you join match.com?"

CHAPTER 13
BREAKING ILLUSIONS & FINDING REALITY

At that time, joining Match.com cost $75. For this fee, the service would display your picture and profile for three months, with membership automatically renewing after the initial period. I joined in February 2012, hoping that maybe I could find someone to help me. In my profile, I wrote only one sentence: "I am looking for someone who will treat me like a princess and love me just the way I am," and I uploaded a single picture.

By January, my email inbox was flooded with about 500 messages from men responding to my profile. On top of this, match.com would also send you *'your match of the day.'* I felt overwhelmed and uninterested, finding most of the profiles insincere. The whole process seemed complicated, so I ignored most of the messages. February turned into March, then April, and I still had not found anyone who interested me.

One week before my membership was set to renew, I decided I needed to cancel as I could not afford to pay for another three months. Then, one day, I received my daily match notification. A picture of a man named James appeared on my screen, and something about it caught my eye. I clicked on his profile and began to read. James's profile was long

Chapter 13: Breaking Illusions & Finding Reality

and detailed. He is a doctor, and his words conveyed a sense of pain and broken-heartedness. His honesty and the depth of his profile intrigued me. The more I read, the more I felt a connection.

So now I saw his picture. Then my friend Nida came home from work, and I showed it to her. I said, "I like this guy, but he did not look at my profile. He is only my match for the day."

On Match.com, you can not communicate directly unless you *'wink'* at someone first. Three days before my membership ended, I winked at him. In the meantime, I did research on my own and verified his name and job just to make sure he was legit. Three days passed without a response, and I began to lose hope.

I told Nida, "I do not think he likes me. He can see that someone winked at him, but he has not bothered to reply."

On the second-to-last day, he winked back. This allowed us to email each other. I quickly emailed him, saying, "Hi, how are you? Please email me at my personal email because you will not see my profile anymore. I am canceling my profile tonight."

By the last day, he still had not replied. I was ready to give up. Nida came home at seven o'clock and I told her, "I need to remove my profile. I do not think he saw my email."

Chapter 13: Breaking Illusions & Finding Reality

She said, "You have another two hours. They will not automatically renew it. You still have time. Wait."

At 9:30 in the evening, he finally emailed me back. He said, "I am so sorry. I am very busy, but I would love to get to know you."

I understood that he must have been busy, given the fact that he is a doctor. I accepted his apology and told him, "Please call me at this number. You will not see my profile anymore. I am canceling it right now."

He called me after five to ten minutes. At that time, I did not have a proper phone number. I was using MagicJack, a device you connect to your desktop to make calls. When we spoke, I apologized for canceling my membership. He asked, "What is this number I am calling?"

I explained, "This is MagicJack."

He asked, "What in the world is MagicJack?"

I said, "It is complicated."

He said, "Okay, I do not think I can call you this way all the time. Do you have a phone?"

I said, "Yes."

Chapter 13: Breaking Illusions & Finding Reality

He replied, "I am going to send you $25 for a phone card so we can talk."

We started talking every day on the phone. Despite never having seen each other, our conversations flowed smoothly, and he seemed genuine and sincere. One day, I took a picture of myself while on the phone with him and sent it to him, saying, "This is me while I am talking to you. Can you do me a favor and take a picture of yourself and send it to me? I am not sure if I am talking to a guy whose picture is 20 years old."

Even though I was desperate to find a husband, I still needed to confirm that this was the same guy as in the profile picture. He sent me a photo, and I was relieved to see he was real. We continued talking every day, like boyfriend and girlfriend. He would call me while driving to the hospital from his home in Dripping Springs. His home was about 2 hours drive from San Antonio, where I lived. By April, after weeks of talking on the phone and messaging like teenagers, we decided to meet.

James had a day off and was not on call on this particular weekend, so he suggested meeting in San Antonio. I was nervous about giving my address to a stranger, but after Googling him and confirming he was real, Nida and I decided it was safe. When the day came, he arrived in a BMW convertible. It was 2012, and I remember the moment clearly. He parked opposite the house, got out of the car. I thought that he looked just like

Chapter 13: Breaking Illusions & Finding Reality

Tom Cruise. Excited, I ran inside, screaming to Nida, "Oh my God, he is so good-looking!"

James was confused wondering why I ran inside. Thinking that maybe I did not like him because I ran in. Nida and the kids, Nico and Gino, came to the door to meet him.

It was the first time James met my extended family in the US He had me book dinner for our first date. I choose a revolving restaurant on the River Walk in San Antonio. We had sometime before our dinner reservation, so we went to a bar in a nearby hotel. Sitting there, thinking to get past the first date jitters, James ordered a very nice Red wine to impress me. He knew I was a wine drinker, preferring Cabernet Sauvignon.

He saw me as an exotic beauty, and I felt special. As we talked, I decided to be straightforward with him. I told him, "I am not looking for fun. This is real life." I was 45 years old at that time and James was 53 years old. He understood where I was coming from and what I meant when I bluntly told him that I was not looking for fun. We were not getting any younger after all. He respected my honesty.

I told him, "I am looking for someone who can take over my responsibilities. I worked all my life in Dubai, took care of my family, and sent my grandkids to Montessori school. Now I need someone who

Chapter 13: Breaking Illusions & Finding Reality

can help me take care of my parents and also help with my financial responsibilities. Can you do that?" Then I asked, "Can you marry me?"

He responded affirmatively, stating that he was divorced. I continued, "I want to bring my family here—my son, my daughter, and my grandchildren. Is this something you can help me with?"

He agreed, and I promised that if he made my family happy, I would remain by his side and do everything I could to make his life happy until his last day.

As we finished our discussion, James called for the waitress so that he could pay for the wine. After much searching, the waitress could not be found. The manager approached us, apologized for the waitress's absence, and told us the bill was on the house. It felt like this was some kind of good sign.

Inside the revolving restaurant, I placed my purse by the window. As we started chatting and chatting, I suddenly realized my purse was now missing. I got scared and asked James where my purse was. A waiter soon retrieved it, and despite the small embarrassment, we enjoyed our first date.

As we were talking and waiting to place our order, a waiter came with a bouquet of roses. James insisted they were not from him. Soon, the waiter returned and sheepishly said he had made a mistake. We laughed

Chapter 13: Breaking Illusions & Finding Reality

it off and continued enjoying our night. Later, James went to the bathroom because with the restaurant revolving, our table rotated away, and he could not find me when he came back. Finally, a couple at another table pointed him in the right direction.

We had met and spent that first magical night together, but we did not sleep together—literally or sexually. I made sure of it. I was not ready to be that vulnerable with him yet. I had too much tension, stress, and worries in my life, so sex was the last thing on my mind. For me, it felt like I was still a virgin, emotionally speaking.

Throughout April, we continued to talk and get to know each other better. James would call me before and after work every day. One day, he told me he had a weekend off and wanted to spend it with me. Usually, he was on call every second weekend, having to go to the hospital on both Saturday and Sunday. He picked me up and took me to Austin, where we checked into a hotel next to his hospital. That was the weekend I finally let my guard down and surrendered to him. From then on, every weekend he was free, he wanted me to be with him.

By May, we decided to move in together. That was when I discovered something I had not expected. James was not yet divorced from his wife. They were separated but nothing was final. He lived in Dripping Springs, in a gated community on a two-acre property. The place was like a resort, with a 6,000-square-foot house and a swimming pool. He also had two

Chapter 13: Breaking Illusions & Finding Reality

dogs. James had two stepchildren with his ex-wife and two children from his first marriage. I was completely unprepared for this situation.

I found myself living in a secluded community, hidden away in the countryside, where my role was less than ideal. Essentially, I had become a mistress, a title I was far from proud of. James, though separated from his wife, was not yet divorced. His marital status confused me initially because I thought he was already divorced when we started our relationship. But as I settled into his home, the reality of the situation became painfully clear.

James's house was a chaotic battleground, caught in the crossfire of a bitter and ongoing divorce. His ex-wife's belongings cluttered the space, serving as a constant reminder of her lingering presence, even though she no longer lived there. Their son, however, still resided in the house, adding to the complexity of our situation. The mess of their lives seemed to spill over into every corner, making me question my place in this fractured household.

Despite the turmoil, James and I were left undisturbed. His ex-wife did not interfere, and they had ceased communication. Yet, in this private, exclusive community, I was very much the "other woman." It was a disorienting reality, and I was grappling to understand my position. I stayed put, navigating the complicated dynamics, while James honored his promise to support my family back in the Philippines. My financial worries were easing, as I was able to send money to my children and grandchildren regularly. My family's situation was improving, and life was gradually becoming more stable.

However, my situation in the United States was still precarious. I still had no legal rights and no papers to secure my stay. James lived in Dripping Springs, a remote area far removed from any semblance of city life. Everything was miles away, and I felt isolated without a car. My only means of identification was my Dubai driving license, which was of no use here. Trapped inside the house most of the time, I felt disconnected from the world outside. James would leave for work early in the morning and return late in the evening, leaving me alone for long stretches of the day.

Despite these challenges, I adapted to my new life. I embraced my social nature, hosting lively parties that became the talk of the neighborhood. When I threw a party, it was a celebration to remember. Many of our friends were musicians, so live music punctuated our gatherings. Soon, we became very popular in the community for our parties. This went on for a year. I refrained from pressing James about his divorce. I feared that pushing the issue might jeopardize the financial support he provided for my family. It was a delicate balance, and I chose to remain silent, observing the situation without confronting it.

Chapter 13: Breaking Illusions & Finding Reality

But as time passed, it became increasingly clear that something needed to change. One year had gone by, and still, no divorce papers had been filed. My patience was wearing thin. I could not ignore the reality any longer. I needed clarity about our future. I finally gathered the courage to ask James about his plans. "Do you have any intention of getting divorced?" I asked him one evening.

His response was evasive, and I sensed that a part of him was still emotionally tied to his ex-wife. This realization hit hard. In the beginning, I suspected that he still harbored feelings for her, and now those suspicions seemed to be validated. Our relationship, which had given me hope and stability, was now shrouded in uncertainty. I felt a knot of anxiety tightening in my chest as I awaited his answer, knowing that our future hinged on his response.

Living in James's house, I unearthed countless surprises when he left me alone. It was as if I was peeling back the layers of a life I had not fully grasped. His home, much like our relationship, was filled with complexities and unexpected twists. Despite my efforts to adapt, my journey with James was anything but smooth. Every step forward seemed to come with its own set of challenges, like navigating a road littered with bumps and turns.

I had no bank account of my own, no access to his finances, and no legal rights in our relationship because we were not married. I was effectively trapped, relying on him for everything. One day, he seemed to recognize my predicament and suggested, "Why do you not drop me off at the hospital and pick me up later? You can use the car in the meantime." He was referring to his BMW convertible, a car that symbolized the freedom I longed for but did not yet have.

His house was a sprawling 6,000 square feet, and I took it upon myself to keep it immaculate. My organizational skills were almost obsessive—friends would joke that my pantry looked more like a grocery store, with everything arranged in alphabetical order. Maintaining the house became a part of my daily routine. My attention to detail was meticulous; it was my way of carving out some semblance of control in a life that often felt chaotic.

We became quite social in the neighborhood, hosting poker nights and other gatherings that brought people into our lives. I met many neighbors and made friends, both individually and as a couple. Our home was known for its lively atmosphere during these events, and I found a sense of community in these interactions. Yet, despite the outward appearances, I could not shake the feeling of being an appendage and not a partner.

One day, the weight of our situation became too much to bear, and I confronted James. "Why are we still like this?" I asked him, my voice tinged with frustration and longing. I could see the regret in his eyes. He

Chapter 13: Breaking Illusions & Finding Reality

knew he had made promises—promises of a life together, of marriage, that remained unfulfilled. But I held back from expressing my disappointment directly, recognizing that he had been supporting me and my family despite everything.

Feeling the pressure, James finally took action. He filed for divorce from his ex-wife. The process began in 2012, shortly after we moved in together, and dragged on until it was finalized in May 2013. I can not recall the exact date, but the relief when the divorce was confirmed was palpable. It marked the end of a difficult chapter for him and the beginning of a new one for us.

Although we had lived together through this period of uncertainty, knowing that his divorce was finalized brought a sense of legitimacy to our relationship. The hurdles we faced together only strengthened our bond. With his past officially behind him, I felt hopeful about our future.

CHAPTER 14
UNDER THE BLAZING SUN

It was the middle of 2013. James's divorce had been finalized back in May, but we were still not married. I was caught in a limbo, worried and insecure about my legal status. The house in Dripping Springs no longer felt like home. James asked if I wanted to stay in the house, but I declined. It was not my dream house; it was a place filled with memories, but it did not feel like my future. We decided to move to the nearby town of Kyle. Here we rented a spacious five-bedroom house. This new chapter in Kyle brought a mix of emotions, especially as my second-to-youngest brother, with Carnival Cruise, would come and visit us. He was the first family member to meet James, and their meeting felt like a bridge between my past and present.

One incident in July or August brought all of my fears to the surface. I was driving James's BMW convertible. He had left me with the car after I dropped him off at work. It was one of those Texas mornings, hot and sunny. I had plans to meet friends for lunch at noon and had left the house around 10:30 AM, dressed in a purple miniskirt, my long, straight hair cascading over my shoulders. I mention this because it plays a significant part in what followed.

Chapter 14: Under The Blazing Sun

Arriving early at 11 AM, I decided to kill some time at the Galleria, a nearby shopping mall. The plan was to park there briefly before heading to the restaurant. As I navigated the exit, I found myself at a busy intersection with 3 lanes: 2 leading right, 1 turn lane and to the left. For me to turn left, I had to cross the first 2 lanes. Both lanes stopped to let me through, but as I moved into the turn lane, a pickup truck came barreling through, hitting the front of James's BMW. The crash was jarring, and the damage to the car's front fender was severe. Shaken, I managed to pull into a gas station by the shoulder while the truck followed and parked behind me.

The driver of the pickup was furious. He jumped out and immediately demanded my insurance and registration. I felt a surge of panic; I had no insurance of my own, and the registration showed James's and his ex-wife's names. My Dubai driving license was my only identification. The driver's anger escalated, and he called the police.

In that moment, fear gripped me like never before. I had no legal standing in the US, no proper documentation, and now I was involved in a traffic accident. Wearing a miniskirt under the sweltering Texas sun, I could feel the sweat trickling down my back as I stood beside the damaged car, my heart racing.

Desperate and unsure of what to do, I broke my usual protocol and called James at his office. He answered, surprised, "What is going on?"

Chapter 14: Under The Blazing Sun

"I have had an accident," I blurted out, my voice trembling. "I am scared. This guy wants my insurance, and I do not have any. What should I do?"

James, trying to calm me down, said, "Stay where you are. Do not leave. I will send you the insurance details. Just wait for the police, whatever you do, do not leave."

Climbing back into the car, I turned on the air conditioning and tried to compose myself. Minutes felt like hours as I waited for the police to arrive. The pickup driver continued to pester me, demanding answers until I rolled up the window and ignored him. My mind raced with worst-case scenarios—getting arrested, being deported, ending up in jail.

After what felt like an eternity, two hours later, the police finally arrived. The officer walked up, immediately apologizing for the delay, explaining he was caught in traffic. The pickup driver wasted no time in laying out his complaints: "She does not have insurance! Her name is not on the registration!"

The officer, however, was unfazed. "I am not talking to you," he told the man, turning his attention to me. "Are you okay?" he asked gently.

I nodded, though my nerves were still frayed. "I really need to use the bathroom," I confessed.

Chapter 14: Under The Blazing Sun

The officer, who seemed to take an interest in my situation, said, "Do not worry, we will sort this out quickly. Can I see your license?"

Handing him my Dubai license, I explained, "I just arrived last week to visit my boyfriend. I live in Dubai."

"Oh, so you are a foreigner!" he said, his tone lightening. "How is Dubai?"

"It is fine," I replied, forcing a smile.

The officer filled out the accident report for me, even flirting a little as he did. He assured me I would not receive a ticket. Relieved but exhausted, I skipped the luncheon and went straight back to the house.

When I recounted the incident to James later that day, he chuckled. "That must have been quite a sight," he said, trying to lighten the mood. The laughter was a brief respite from the growing uncertainties in my life. It was a reminder of how tenuous my situation was—without papers, without rights, and now, without the illusion of the stability I had tried so hard to maintain.

Time passed after the accident, and while things returned to a semblance of normalcy, a nagging concern lingered. James's divorce was finalized, yet he had not mentioned marriage to me. Two years had

Chapter 14: Under The Blazing Sun

slipped by since I arrived in the United States, and I was still without legal papers. Every day felt precarious, living under the shadow of deportation.

On December 29, 2013, I was taking a shower, lost in thought and prayer. I was grateful for James's support—he provided shelter, sent money to my family, took care of my grandkids and parents, and gave me an allowance. But despite my gratitude, a persistent fear gnawed at me: *what if I pushed too hard and he sent me away?* I had no Plan B, no fallback. At that moment, under the cascade of warm water, I found a flicker of courage. I asked for strength to broach the topic that had been haunting me.

With my hair still damp, I walked into the kitchen where James was sitting at our small table nook. "We need to talk," I said, my voice trembling slightly.

He looked up, curious. "What about?"

Gathering my nerve, I sat across from him. "Do you have plans to marry me?"

James seemed taken aback but composed himself quickly. "Of course," he replied.

"When?" I pressed, feeling the weight of my question hang in the air.

He hesitated before saying, "When my life is fixed."

Chapter 14: Under The Blazing Sun

His words hit me hard. I felt a rush of frustration and desperation. "Are you kidding me? Since we decided to live together, our lives have been one. While you are fixing your life, what about mine?"

James looked at me, seemingly at a loss. "But I do not have a ring," he said finally.

"Wait here," I said, determined to resolve this once and for all. I went to the bedroom, retrieved my jewelry box, and returned to the kitchen. Placing the box in front of him, I said, "Pick a ring."

James opened the box, selected a ring, and held it gently. He whispered, "Will you marry me?"

"What?" I asked, hardly believing what I was hearing.

"Will you marry me?" he repeated softly.

It was a surreal, unexpected and decidedly unromantic moment. "Yes," I said, a smile spreading across my face as he slid the ring onto my finger. It was December 29, just before lunch. I was so thrilled that I immediately posted a picture of my hand on Facebook, announcing, "We are engaged." I called my mother and daughter to share the news—everyone was ecstatic.

As New Year's Eve approached, we attended a gala party, excited to celebrate our engagement. The next day, January 1, 2014, everything was

Chapter 14: Under The Blazing Sun

closed for the holiday. But on January 2, as James was preparing to go back to work, I told him, "Before you leave, we have to go to the courthouse."

"The courthouse?" he asked, puzzled. "What for?"

"We are going to get a marriage license," I replied with newfound assertiveness.

We headed to the courthouse, obtained our marriage license, and learned that in Texas, the license needed to be advertised for a month to allow any objections. James seemed to think this would delay the wedding indefinitely. However, I had a simple plan in mind. We would wed on February 14, Valentine's Day.

I planned a simple wedding to take place in our home. I had arranged for Nida to be my maid of honor and invited a few close friends. We called a lawyer friend to officiate. In an intimate ceremony at home, surrounded by close friends, James and I exchanged vows. It was a modest, heartfelt wedding.

The next morning, February 15, our lawyer friend realized he had forgotten to have us sign the marriage certificate. We hurried to the nearby CVS pharmacy, of all places, to complete the paperwork. Officially married, we signed the certificate amidst the mundane hustle of the store.

Chapter 14: Under The Blazing Sun

With our marriage official, the next step was to secure my legal status. I needed a driving license, a Social Security number, and, most importantly, a green card. As an overstaying immigrant, applying for these on my own was not an option. I told James, "We need to hire an immigration lawyer."

We found one, paying $5,000 to handle everything from filing documents to securing my green card. The process stretched from March through the summer of 2014. The final step is the interview. It was here that we sat down with an immigration officer, and he asked us questions to prove the legitimacy of our marriage. By August, my green card was finally released. I was elated and wasted no time in converting my Dubai license to a US driving license.

We had married in Kyle, Texas, and now, I was officially and legally part of James's life. The whirlwind journey of anxiety, hope, and determination had led me to this moment. With legal status secured and a future with James solidified, I finally felt a sense of stability that had eluded me for so long.

On December 13, 2014, a phone call shattered the calm of our newly settled life. My younger brother called with devastating news: our father had passed away. The loss was profound, and the timing was complicated. Without my green card, I was at risk of being unable to attend the funeral.

Chapter 14: Under The Blazing Sun

Thankfully, having recently secured my green card, I could book a flight to Manila. I booked a flight and headed out the next day, December 14.

Flying to Manila was a somber journey. My heart was heavy as I returned to bury my father. The loss was a stark reminder of the fragility of life and the importance of family. After the funeral, I returned to Texas, where James and I resumed our life in Kyle. James had missed meeting my father before he passed, a regret that weighed on both of us. However, in 2018, we visited the Philippines together for Christmas. It was an emotional trip; James finally met my mother, and he reconnected with my brother Eric, who had also visited us in Texas. He was also able to meet the rest of my family in person. Our blended lives felt more complete after that visit.

Back in Texas, though, life still had its challenges. The state did not seem to fit us. I found Texas to be harsh, and as much as we tried to make it work, the feeling of belonging never fully settled in. I longed for a change and began dreaming of living in Florida. We started searching for opportunities, and I actively helped James by sending his CV to various agencies.

In early 2015, our search led us to an intriguing prospect: an interview for James in Oklahoma City. We were hopeful, but little did I know the adventure and anxiety that awaited us there. Interviews in

Chapter 14: Under The Blazing Sun

Oklahoma City were unique; they insisted the spouse accompany the candidate to help convince the family to move.

So, we went to Oklahoma City. While James attended his interview, a realtor took me on a tour of potential houses. The city was entirely foreign to me. As we walked through one of the houses, the realtor showed me a curious feature in the garage: a door leading into the floor.

"What is that?" I asked, puzzled.

"This is a plus for the house," she explained. "If there is a tornado, it is a safe place to hide."

Instead of feeling reassured, I felt a wave of unease. I had no experience with such natural calamities. The only significant disaster I could recall was the eruption of Mount Pinatubo in the Philippines, which was far from where I lived. In Dubai, the closest thing to a natural calamity was a sandstorm, which I was also far removed from. The concept of a tornado was utterly alien to me.

Suddenly, a loud siren blared, startling me. "What is that?" I asked, alarmed.

"Oh, it is normal here. They are testing the tornado sirens," the realtor said casually. It dawned on me that Oklahoma City was on the boundary

Chapter 14: Under The Blazing Sun

of what is called Tornado Alley, an area where tornados are very frequent. This was a fact I was wholly unprepared for.

I returned to James, who was seated at a long table with other Doctors and their spouses. As we exchanged glances, the siren blared again. One of the wives, noticing my discomfort, said reassuringly, "Do not worry about it. You will get used to it."

But I could not imagine getting used to such a thing. That evening, back at the hotel, I had a serious conversation with James. "Okay, babe," I said, "If you accept this job, I will go home to the Philippines every six months and stay here for just a month at a time. I can not live here permanently."

The prospect of tornadoes and the constant anxiety they brought were too much for me to bear. I realized that while seeking new opportunities was essential, finding a place that felt like home, where we both felt safe and comfortable, was just as crucial.

After the unsettling experience in Oklahoma City, fate took a more promising turn the next day. James was in the middle of another interview when his phone started ringing. He could not answer it immediately, as he was deep in discussions, but later that evening, back at the hotel, he saw the missed call was from Florida.

Chapter 14: Under The Blazing Sun

Intrigued, I urged him to return the call. It turned out to be the partner of a large cardiology group in Florida, an Indian man also married to a Filipina. He was reaching out to offer an interview. As they talked, it became clear that this could be the opportunity we were waiting for.

"Please come over for an interview," he had said, his familiarity with our background adding a personal touch to the conversation. Excited by this prospect, we scheduled a visit. By mid-February 2015, James and I found ourselves in Florida for the interview. They had generously arranged for us to stay three nights, allowing us to explore both the company and the local area.

Our time there was memorable. I visited Disney World for the first time—a magical experience that brought a much-needed sense of joy and adventure. One evening, the company treated us to dinner at a Chinese restaurant, where I met the team: four Indians, a Pakistani, a Korean, and an American. They were a diverse and friendly group, and their warmth made us feel welcome. The decision became clear—Florida was calling.

We returned to Texas with a renewed purpose. Oklahoma was no longer an option; our future lay in Florida. Over the next few months—May, June, and July—we packed up our lives in Texas. By August 2015, we had rented a house in Windermere, a beautiful suburb of Orlando, and moved there.

Chapter 14: Under The Blazing Sun

James could not start his new job immediately. He needed to obtain a Florida license to practice, which took about a month. During this waiting period, we began settling into our new home, embracing the opportunities that lay ahead.

In 2016, we found a charming three-bedroom house and decided to buy it. Building the house from the ground up was an exciting journey, and moving into our first home in Windermere felt like a significant milestone. Life became smoother, more settled.

Yet, my dream of living by water persisted. I never stopped searching for a property that offered that serene lakefront view. Windermere, known for its affluent residents like Tiger Woods and Shaquille O'Neal, was desirable but costly. Our house was outside the exclusive area called Isleworth—where the wealthy resided—but still close enough to enjoy the perks of the location.

In 2017, after relentless searching, I found a lake property situated between Lake Van and Lake Alfred. It was remote, about an hour from the city, yet close enough to Disney World and Universal Studios to retain a connection to the vibrant Orlando life. The property was a little over a quarter of an acre and nestled in a quiet, serene location—my perfect sanctuary.

James was initially hesitant. "Are you sure you want to live out here?" he asked, concerned about the distance from the city.

Chapter 14: Under The Blazing Sun

"Yes," I said, confident. "It is my serenity. I love it."

We bought the property in 2017 but decided to wait before building our house, planning to create our dream home when the time was right. The lot sat peacefully, waiting for us to be ready.

As life settled into a rhythm in Florida, unexpected news from Dubai shattered the tranquility. In October 2018, my niece tearfully called to deliver devastating news—my brother Roy, who had remained in Dubai after my departure in 2010, had passed away.

My heart sank as I listened to her explain the circumstances. Roy had suffered a sudden heart attack at a train station in Dubai. Despite efforts to save him at Rashid Hospital, he had passed away. The news left us reeling; the reality of his absence was difficult to accept.

For three days, Roy's body remained in the hospital morgue as my nieces faced the harsh reality of the situation. They lacked the funds needed to release his body for transport back to the Philippines, where they wished to lay him to rest. The hospital required $5,000 for the release and transportation costs—a daunting sum that seemed impossible at the time.

With no cash on hand, I turned to my network of friends, sharing our plight privately on Facebook. It was a moment of vulnerability, asking for help for the sake of my dear brother. The response was overwhelming.

Chapter 14: Under The Blazing Sun

Within a week, the generosity of friends—some contributing $500, others $50 or $100—enabled us to gather the necessary funds. We arranged for Roy's body to be released, placed in a coffin, and transported to the Philippines. My nieces accompanied their father on his final journey home.

Once in the Philippines, I ensured everything was prepared for Roy's funeral. It was a heartbreaking time, made more painful by the fact that I could not be there physically to support my nieces in their grief. I urged them not to wait for my return but to proceed with the arrangements as planned.

Life continued to unfold. In 2019, before the pandemic altered global travel, James and I had plans to visit Dubai and the Philippines. I had traveled to Dubai in March 2020, with James intending to join me shortly after. However, as the pandemic escalated, flights were grounded, and borders closed. James made the difficult decision not to travel, concerned about getting stranded abroad. He urged me to return home, prompting a rush to change my flight amidst the chaos of airport closures and escalating ticket prices.

Within a few days, I was safely back in Florida, where the reality of the pandemic set in. Like the rest of the world, we faced the uncertainty of lockdowns and plans put on hold indefinitely. But as 2021 dawned,

Chapter 14: Under The Blazing Sun

there was a glimmer of hope. Vaccines offered a path forward, and slowly but surely, life began to regain a sense of normality.

CHAPTER 15
A PANDEMIC TWIST

In March 2020, Jim and I were excitedly planning our long-awaited trip to Dubai and the Philippines. On March 10th, I flew to Dubai, with Jim scheduled to join me on the 14th. It was my first time back in Dubai after ten years, having left in 2010. The reunion with my niece and nephew was heartwarming. We celebrated by going out and enjoying the city, reminiscing about old times and catching up on all that had happened in the past decade.

My first night in Dubai was filled with joy. I took my niece and nephew out, along with several other relatives—all now grown up, aged between 21 and 27. We had a fantastic time, and I also reunited with my dear friend, Lynn, who showed me around. The following day, I indulged in some shopping, treating myself to some gold jewelry, a cherished souvenir from Dubai.

However, our plans were abruptly interrupted. Jim called me with troubling news—flights from Europe to the United States were being suspended due to the worsening COVID-19 pandemic. He did not want to risk getting stuck in another country and urged me to return home. The dream of a two-week holiday in Dubai and the Philippines vanished,

Chapter 15: A Pandemic Twist

replaced by a scramble to change my flight. Despite already paying a significant amount for our business class tickets, Emirates Airlines charged an additional $700 just to change the date of my return flight. The airport was chaotic, with many people desperately trying to get back to their home countries.

I returned to the US, where the situation was equally dire. By the end of March, everything was shutting down—shops, offices, schools. The only people who continued to work tirelessly were those in both essential services, including the medical field, such as my husband. The atmosphere was tense, compounded by increasing racial tensions and incidents of violence against Asian communities. The news was filled with stories of suffering and loss, from the pandemic's devastating impact in Italy to the senseless acts of hate closer to home.

One morning, as Jim came downstairs, he found me crying at the kitchen counter. The weight of the world's troubles felt unbearable. Seeing the news about an Asian father and son being beaten due to racial hatred was heart-wrenching. Jim gently advised me to stop watching the news, recognizing the toll it was taking on my emotional well-being.

The pandemic also kept me from my usual trips to the Philippines. Since my father's passing, I made it a point to visit regularly, but 2020 marked the second year I could not go home. Not seeing my mother and family added to the emotional strain. When Jim came home from work,

Chapter 15: A Pandemic Twist

he took every precaution to protect us, often isolating himself to avoid potential exposure. The fear of this unknown virus, without a vaccine or treatment in sight, was overwhelming.

As the months passed—March, April, May, June—the world slowly adjusted to the new normal. By mid-2020, there was talk of vaccines, bringing a glimmer of hope. Life began to regain some semblance of order, though it was far from normal.

Amidst the chaos, we decided to start building our long-awaited dream house. We had purchased a beautiful lake-front property outside of Orlando in 2017 but had not yet started construction. Despite feeling a pang of guilt as many faced job losses, we seized the opportunity presented by low interest rates and began building in November 2020. Our new home, a custom-designed haven on the shores of Lake Alfred, symbolized a fresh start.

The location was perfect—Lake Alfred to the east provided stunning sunrises that we could enjoy from our backyard. A new chapter had begun, marked by resilience and hope for a brighter future.

Every morning, the sunrise greeted me in our bedroom, painting the sky with hues of orange and pink. This house was our labor of love. From breaking ground in November, we spent eight months building it. I was there at least three times a week, supervising every detail. Jim and I

Chapter 15: A Pandemic Twist

designed everything from scratch, making this house our dream home, our baby.

The process was stressful, but it was worth it. Feng Shui principles guided me, ensuring the house had the right energy flow. This was our second home. Our first, a small three-bedroom house, was bought to accommodate my daughter and her four kids for when they arrived in the US. This new house was a testament to our hard work and dreams.

In August 2021, we moved in, and shortly after, I called my mother on Messenger. Despite our differences, I wanted to share my joy with her. For the first time, I heard her say she was proud of me. It was a moment I had longed for, a validation of all my efforts. I invited her to visit, but she declined, saying she could not live without neighbors and the bustling life she was used to back home. Our new neighborhood was quiet and serene, quite the contrast to the lively streets of the Philippines.

Around the same time, in March or April of 2021, my daughter's visa was approved. With this, we began preparing to welcome her and my four grandkids to the US. It was a busy year, juggling the completion of our new home and preparing for my family's arrival.

Before leaving the country, they needed medical exams to come to the USA. My youngest granddaughter was three years old and was already an American citizen. As such, she did not need the exam, while

Chapter 15: A Pandemic Twist

my other grandchildren, ages 13, 16, and 17, all needed the exam. After this, they were ready for the long trip to the US.

When September rolled around, I decided to celebrate my birthday with a housewarming party. In just six months, I had hosted five parties, quickly becoming known in the neighborhood for my hospitality. However, the joy was short-lived. In mid-September, my younger brother called me with devastating news. "Ate, Ma is gone," he said. It was September 10 or 11, 2021. My elder brother started to explain, but I cut him off, needing to know what had happened to our mother.

She had been found dead in her home after neighbors noticed a foul smell. Living in a compound with my brother but in separate apartments, no one had checked on her for several days.

They found my mother in a tragic position, kneeling down as if she had tried to get up but could not. She had fallen, her head touching the floor, and given her weight, it must have been impossible for her to rise. I was desperate to go home to bury her, but with COVID-19, there was a 10-day quarantine required at the airport in the Philippines before you could enter the country. This made it unfeasible for me to travel.

In our tradition, we do not do cremations; we have open caskets so the family can see their loved ones and say their goodbyes. But the pandemic had changed everything. Even though my mother did not die of COVID-19, all bodies had to be cremated. My heart bled because I

Chapter 15: A Pandemic Twist

could not see her one last time. The last time I saw her was during that video call, and she had been so proud of me. It felt like a premonition, a final moment of connection before she passed.

Her urn was kept in our house in the Philippines for a year. This time was one of the saddest periods of my life.

I instructed my brothers to call a priest immediately to bless our mother's soul before touching her body. The quarantine restrictions in the Philippines were still high, unlike in the US, which made the situation even more complicated. The realization that my mother had passed away alone, unnoticed for days, was heartbreaking.

As I navigated the grief of losing my mother, I could not help but reflect on our relationship and the brief moment of connection we had just before her passing. Despite the sadness, I found a small comfort in knowing that she had seen our new home and expressed her pride in me. It was a bittersweet end to an emotional chapter.

In 2022, after our initial plans to visit Dubai and Philippines in 2020 were canceled due to the Pandemic, we finally made the trip to Dubai and Egypt instead. It was Jim's first time to visit the Middle East, and it was an amazing experience. We returned to the US and focused on settling in our new home.

Chapter 15: A Pandemic Twist

In September 2022, my daughter and her children arrived in the USA and came to live in our house located in Windermere, Florida. We combined their welcome to the US party and my birthday on September 26. It was a celebration of all our hard work and achievements, as well as a chance to introduce my daughter and my grandkids to our circle of friends.

We again celebrated with a Christmas party on December 10, 2022, introducing my daughter and grandkids to our neighbors and other friends. It was a period of transitions and new beginnings, marked by the deep loss of my mother but also the joy of family reunions and new opportunities.

CHAPTER 16
THE FIRE THAT CHANGED EVERYTHING

On December 10th, I had just wrapped up my Christmas party at home. A few days later, on December 13th, something strange happened. This day was my father's death anniversary, and somehow, I felt a sense of premonition about it.

Early that morning, at around 2:00 AM, our smoke detector went off, making a loud noise. My husband and I were startled awake by an obnoxious noise. He got up to check what was wrong, but just as he was about to investigate, the alarm suddenly stopped. We were puzzled but decided to go back to bed.

At about 5:30 AM, the same thing happened again. The smoke detector blared loudly, waking us up once more. We were tempted to ignore it, but since my husband usually wakes up at 6:30 AM, we decided to check it out. Again, as we were about to do something, the alarm stopped on its own. We were baffled by this strange occurrence, but since the alarm did not go off again, we decided to leave it alone. My husband got ready and went to work, and the rest of the day passed without any issues.

Chapter 16: The Fire That Changed Everything

Later that afternoon, I called the electrician from our neighborhood who had installed the smoke detectors. He came over and checked every single one of them—there are about 12 in the house—but found nothing wrong.

The next day, December 14th, I lit a candle in the house to honor my father's death anniversary. My husband followed his usual routine and went to work. Every day for the past 12 years, he texts me around 6:00 or 6:30 PM when he has finished work, letting me know he is on his way home. After I received his message, I replied that I would start preparing dinner. It usually takes him about an hour to drive home from Kissimmee or Saint Cloud, so I time my preparations accordingly.

On that day, when he texted me, I still had some time, so I decided to go to our gym and do some yoga. I was wearing my yoga pants and a bralette, with my hair tied up. While exercising, I kept an eye on the time and noticed that I only had about half an hour left. I finished my yoga session around 7:00 PM and went outside to the lanai to turn on the gas grill.

As I did every day, I turned on the two burners and set the temperature to 400 degrees so it would be ready for grilling. While waiting for the grill to heat up, I started preparing an avocado salad. I had just started with the salad when my husband arrived home. I told him, "Okay, babe, your dinner will be ready in 15 to 20 minutes." He

Chapter 16: The Fire That Changed Everything

responded, "Okay, I will not shower, but I will exercise first." He then changed into his workout clothes and headed to the gym while I continued preparing dinner.

After finishing the salad, I grabbed the ribeye in my right hand and went outside to check the grill. I placed the ribeye down next to the grill and opened the lid to see if the temperature was ready. When I opened the grill, there was no heat or flame. I did not smell anything abnormal—no propane at all—even though both burners were switched on for about fifteen minutues. Confused, I switched them off and called out to my husband, "Babe, there is no flame." But he did not hear me because he was doing his floor exercises, completely focused and unaware of what was happening outside.

Since I did not smell anything strange after about five seconds, I decided to switch the burners back on. The moment I did, the grill exploded. Apparently, the gas had been on and propane had been accumulating inside for about fifteen minutes. When I turned the grill back on, it ignited with a thunderous bang that my husband heard from inside. The flame did not shoot out from above. It seems that propane is heavier than air, so it accumulated below the grill. As a result, the flame came from below and wrapped around my body, burning me for what felt like an eternity, but in reality, it was just a few seconds.

Chapter 16: The Fire That Changed Everything

As the flames engulfed me, I screamed for help. My husband, thinking I might be doing some last-minute Christmas decorations and suffered an accident, rushed into the living room. There, he saw me. I was standing in the lanai, with my arms spread out like I was on a cross, screaming in pain. My clothes had melted onto my body. He quickly rushed me to the bathroom. He did not throw me into the swimming pool but instead put me under a very cold shower.

As I stood there under the cold water, I kept touching my face, crying out, "My face, my face, my face!" My husband reassured me that my face was not badly burned, but the damage was already done. When he tried to remove my melted clothes, my skin came off with them, especially from my legs, where my spandex yoga pants had melted onto my body. The only part of my clothing that did not completely melt was the fabric behind the bralette and the shoes I had on.

The worst burns were on my stomach and legs, which had been exposed because of the bralette. My arms were covered in blisters, and my hair was singed on the right side. My lips and face had first-degree burns, but they were still incredibly painful. My arms were covered in second-degree burns, and stomach and legs had third-degree burns.

After helping me out of the shower, my husband dressed me in a single-piece pullover dress. He did not take me to the local hospital. He drove me to one of the largest hospitals in Orlando, Celebration Hospital,

Chapter 16: The Fire That Changed Everything

where he practices. He wanted to make sure I received the best possible care.

The drive from our house to Celebration Hospital took about 45 minutes. I was in so much pain, holding one hand to the handle on the side door of the car and the other to my husband's hand, crying the whole way. I kept telling him how painful it was, but neither of us knew the extent of the damage yet.

When we arrived at Celebration Hospital, there was no one to attend to me right away. We had to manage on our own. My husband parked the car in front of the ER (Emergency Room) and tried to help me into a wheelchair. I could not move properly; my legs and arms were spread out because I had no skin left to hold everything together. I was shaking uncontrollably.

A nurse seeing us finally took me straight to an examination room, where the doctor promptly attended to me. She immediately recognized the severity of the burns, since the hospital did not have a burn unit. They stabilized me and called for a helicopter to air evac me to the nearest hospital with a burn unit. The pain was indescribable; my whole body shook with tremors. At that point, they knocked me out with Dlaudid. After this, I do not recall much.

My husband later told me that they flew me by helicopter from Celebration Hospital to Orlando Health in downtown Orlando. This is

Chapter 16: The Fire That Changed Everything

where the only burn unit in the area is located. When I arrived, they immediately took me to a procedure room, cleaned my burns, and then covered me in sterilized gauze. The doctor told my husband that I would likely be in the hospital for about three months and that I might need up to five surgeries. He also told my husband that if this were to happen twenty years ago, I would not survive. I was unaware of all this at the time.

The doctor also told my husband to call our family. The burn was very extensive, I had third-degree burns over 41% of my body. This means 41% of my body was no longer covered with skin. When the doctor told my husband to call our family, he reached out to my brothers in the Philippines, as my parents had already passed away. But before that, he called my daughter, who had just moved to the US, and then my son, who was in the Philippines. When my husband explained what had happened, my children were confused and did not understand how I could have been burned so badly. They initially thought I had been in a car accident. My daughter, Mickie, was especially confused, struggling to make sense of what had happened to me. Fortunately, my husband, being a doctor, knew how to talk to them and help them understand and manage the emotional trauma they were experiencing.

I was in the intensive care burn unit, which also doubled as the trauma unit for eight days. I had no idea what was happening around me as I was heavily medicated to control the pain. Each day, they needed to

Chapter 16: The Fire That Changed Everything

clean my burns to help prevent infection. This was a painful and grueling process. They used a sterile towel to scrub the burns. It took six people—three on each side of me—three hours to clean and dress my burns. This process was repeated every day until I was discharged.

On the first day, the doctors gave me 20 milligrams of morphine to help me get through the painful scrubbing process, a typical dose is only 2 to 5 milligrams. Despite this, the pain was still unbearable. When the nurses came to change my dressings, they would play my favorite music at a very high volume to try to distract me. An hour before they started, they would give me oral *OxyContin* and then I.V. Morphine during the scraping. Despite this, massive doses of narcotics it still was not enough.

Once they started, they closed the door, and my husband and daughter had to wait outside for three hours. The morphine was given to me bit by bit, and I was asked to hold the hands of the nurses on either side of me. Even with all this, the pain was indescribable, and I could not scream—I just cried. One of the nurses encouraged me to scream, saying it would help, but instead, I prayed, repeating the Hail Mary over and over for the entire three hours while they scrubbed my burns.

The nursing team could not stand to see me in so much pain. On the second day, a nurse named Dale suggested adding *Versed* with the morphine to help with the pain control. This medication, when combined with morphine, could have dangerous side effects. My husband had to

Chapter 16: The Fire That Changed Everything

sign a consent form agreeing to its use, which he did, knowing otherwise, the pain would kill me. I was in the ICU for eight days and in the hospital for a total of five weeks. Every day was a battle. The pain medication left me so drugged up that I do not remember much of what happened.

Routine visitors were not allowed, and my room was kept very clean due to the risk of infection. Given that 41% of my body was basically an open wound. For eight days, I was in this state. Every day, a priest would visit, someone would read to me, or they would sing for me. It felt like I was close to death every day. My husband stayed by my side the entire time, and my daughter was there, too, even though she had a three-year-old daughter herself. I do not know what would have happened to me if my daughter had not been there when I had the accident. My husband was there with me every day and spent many nights with me.

While I was in the ICU, the doctors closely monitored my blood pressure, checked my sugar, and watched for infection. Thankfully, I had no complications, so they could focus solely on treating my burns. Despite the trauma I experienced, I kept sharing my progress on Facebook because I wanted people to know how difficult the journey was but also that recovery is possible. If you saw me now, you would see a happy, cheerful person, even though deep down, I remained psychologically scarred from the reality of what happened.

Chapter 16: The Fire That Changed Everything

On the second day, when they gave me that stronger pain medication, I could not remember the pain during the dressings, but I knew it was there. I could feel it after the dressings were done. Imagine the pain of burning your knuckles and then having to clean them—now imagine that pain covering 41% of your body, from your chest down to your feet.

Even while lying in bed, my mind was strong, telling me to keep moving. I knew that if I did not move, the scars that were forming would contract, and I would not be able to move properly. Despite having no skin and being covered in bandages, with pain reaching down to my bones, I forced myself to exercise as best I could every single day. My brain kept telling me, "You cannot be disabled." At that time, the only part of me my husband could hold was my hand. There was no place on my body left untouched. They had a difficult time finding a place for taking blood pressure or drawing blood. For IV access, they had to place the IV in the jugular vein in my neck. They fed me through a tube inserted through my nose and down my throat into my stomach. I felt like a rag doll, barely holding on.

But every day, I kept going. My daughter would visit, and I would smile for her. My husband would come, and I had to smile for him, too. I took pictures of the sunrise from my hospital room and tried to keep track of time. My only movements were between the bed and a chair. I had a heart monitor attached to me, and if I removed it, the monitor would flatline, but no one would rush in because they knew Mrs. Warren had

Chapter 16: The Fire That Changed Everything

just gone to the bathroom. I tried to do everything on my own—even changing my own bed sheets and gown. I hardly ever ask for help. I was determined to be as independent and normal as possible. I was trying to pretend that nothing had happened to my skin.

During that time, which was around Christmas and New Year, my only strength came from my mind. One day, I held my husband's hand and told him, "Babe, I can not do this anymore. My body is in so much pain, and I can not imagine going through another day." Every day, when the nurses came in to change my dressings, my body would start shaking and I would start crying in anticipation. I dreaded seeing those six people in their yellow gowns approaching me. If I could have pushed them away, I would have. The worst part was when the day nurse would change shifts with the night nurse—it felt like the nightmare was never-ending.

My husband worked long hours, 5 to 12 days straight, and he lost so much weight during that time. After work, he would come straight to my hospital bed, sit beside me, and hold my hand. My daughter told me that every night, he would cry next to me. He was not ready to lose me, and I knew that. I prayed every night, asking God to give me the strength to endure the pain that was tearing apart both my body and my soul. Through all of this, I realized just how much my husband loves me—he never left my side, just like my daughter and grandkids. Their support is the reason I am still alive. I thank God for the unwavering support my family gave me.

Chapter 16: The Fire That Changed Everything

My best friend, Lisa, who lives in Las Vegas, is a huge fan of the football player Tom Brady. She knew his last season was coming to an end, and she, her son and me had planned to come visit in December, around the 15th or 16^{th,} so they could watch him play in Tampa. I was already in the hospital by then. Normally, whenever she would fly to Florida, we would message each other constantly. But this time, she sensed something was wrong because I was not texting her back. Still, they made their way to Florida, took an Uber from the airport, and came straight to my house.

When they arrived, she knew something was off as soon as my husband opened the door. The moment he saw her, he broke down and told her about my accident. My daughter helped take care of Lisa and my family made sure she was driven to Tampa as planned. But she was not about to leave me alone and came to visit me in the ICU.

Lisa and I bonded so much during that time. She was the first person to hold my hand after my first surgery. By then, I was already trying to walk, moving up and down the hospital halls. I documented everything because I initially wanted to share my journey. But eventually, I decided to keep it private so no one could see what happened next.

During those early days in the hospital, only a very few people were allowed to see me while I was in the ICU. Lisa was one of those few, and her presence meant the world to me.

CHAPTER 17
PAIN, PATIENCE, AND PERSEVERANCE

The second surgery I had was a long six-hour procedure. The doctors had to graft new skin on both my legs and stomach. The skin in these places had been literally burned away. There was a large area, about 10 to 15 inches wide, across my abdomen from my left side to my right side, with no skin at all. The doctors told me they would take thin graft from my back to cover these areas.

Instead of taking all the skin at once. It was removed in strips which were about two or three inches wide and eighteen inches long. It was then cut into a mesh and placed over the burned area, one strip at a time. It was a very meticulous work, which is why the surgery took so long. While I was in surgery, everyone was waiting anxiously for me to come out.

When I finally woke up, I was sitting up because I could not lie down on my back. Literally, I was burned on my front and skinned on my back; sleep was almost impossible. If I tried to sit, my stomach would crunch, causing pain, and lying on my back was excruciating. I was monitored very closely to make sure the grafts took the only blessing. During this

Chapter 17: Pain, Patience, and Perseverance

period, the daily scrubbing of the burned areas ceased and they could not risk disturbing the grafts.

My husband came and tried to comfort me, but I do not remember much because I was so heavily medicated. After the surgery, they put a large bandage on my back, covering from my shoulders down to my upper butt. The bandage was black or gray and had a bit of foam in it. The foam helped to keep the bandage from sticking to the donor sites on my back. They also taped the corners of the bandage to help keep it in place.

Once they were sure I was stable, they moved me to a private room where I could have visitors again, though there were still many restrictions—like no flowers allowed. The nurses had to dress my wounds again, but unlike before, they did not scrub them anymore. Instead of using a face towel to scrub off dead skin, they had to be extra careful with the new skin grafts. They cleaned my burns very gently to avoid dislodging in the grafted skin. If the grafts were damaged, there would be no replacement. I had no more donor sites available.

I remember this part very clearly. The pain was intense, and I screamed loudly. The tape on my back was so sticky that they could not remove it easily. They did not use water or anything to loosen it. Every time they tried to pull the tape off, my skin would stick to it. There were two nurses working together to remove it, and I was begging them to stop.

Chapter 17: Pain, Patience, and Perseverance

Imagine I was sitting there, holding my stomach, while they tried to remove the tape so they could clean the area. They were not even removing it completely—just enough to clean it before putting it back on. The pain was so unbearable that I told my husband I could not take it anymore. It was the kind of pain that made you wish you were not alive.

What made it even worse was that they were trying to do this while giving me less morphine. I begged them to give me something for the pain before they started, but it seemed like they were in a hurry. Maybe they needed to go home or finish their shift, but it felt like they were rushing through it. That experience was one of the hardest things I went through in the hospital.

I was terrified of anyone coming near me to touch my back, especially after the pain I went through when they tried to remove the tape that was stuck to my wound. The doctor insisted they had to keep treating the wound because it was still open, and if anything stuck to it, it could cause serious problems. They tried to convince me to let them clean it by just wiping a cream on my back, like the numbing cream a dentist uses. It felt like they were telling me to stop complaining and get through it so they could go home. My husband kept telling me how brave I was for enduring everything, not just the burns but also the psychological pain and fear.

Chapter 17: Pain, Patience, and Perseverance

That first week in the hospital was incredibly tough, and I still had many weeks to go. After coming out of surgery and the ICU, I could not lie down because my back had no skin. I had to sit up in bed, and they told me I needed to consume 3,500 calories a day to aid in my body's attempt to heal. But eating was impossible for me—eating was the last thing I wanted to do. So they put a long tube down through my nose and into my stomach. Through this, they continuously fed me the nutrition I needed every day. They monitored me to make sure I had no complications, but I was so drugged up that I barely knew what was happening around me.

The pain was my constant companion, and my body had become so numb that I just accepted it as part of my life. My bed was always soaking wet. It is one of those things you never consider, but your skin is what keeps all the water inside of you. Without it, you constantly ooze liquid, which quickly soaks through any dressing. I would change my gown two or three times a day, even though it was excruciatingly hard to get up. The daily routine became almost unbearable, but I just pushed through it. Visitors came and went, and my hospital room became a sort of hangout for the nursing staff, especially around Christmas.

I had three nurses who took care of me with a lot of compassion. One of them, Anthony, was a young nurse in his early twenties. He became one of my favorites, though remembering his name was difficult because of all the medication I was on. Anthony was one of the nurses who helped

Chapter 17: Pain, Patience, and Perseverance

with my dressings, but not every day was the same. Sometimes, I had nurses who did not care much about my pain when they removed the bandages, which made the experience even more difficult.

Every night, I would ask my daughter to find out who my night nurse would be because I was always scared. The day nurses seemed more compassionate and caring, but the night nurses were different—less compassionate in my experience. Every night, I feared what might happen next.

Every day, I had a physical therapist come in to help me exercise my legs and arms. My legs were bandaged from top to bottom, and they would stretch them slowly, just as much as I could handle. This daily routine was necessary because the bandages had to be changed regularly, which they called "dressing."

Each day, a different therapist would work with me. The people in the rehabilitation center were very kind and always encouraged me to keep going, asking if I could walk or try different exercises. Despite being one of the worst burn victims there, I was also one of the most active. There were many other trauma patients in the unit, including people who had been in car accidents or had burns, but my injuries were among the most severe. Though my face only looked sunburnt, from my legs up to under my bra and on my arms, the burns were extensive. My arms had second-degree burns, and my skin looked damaged, like a worn-out mop.

Chapter 17: Pain, Patience, and Perseverance

Every day, I had to get up and walk, holding my stomach because of the pain. Walking was excruciating, but I pushed through it, even climbing stairs after two weeks in the hospital. Climbing was especially difficult because it meant bending my legs, causing the burned skin on the back of my legs to rub against each other. The pain was intense, but I ignored it, focusing instead on my recovery and my goal of returning to my normal life. I wanted to be able to run, do yoga, and dance again.

One day, all my grandkids visited me, including my three-year-old granddaughter, Maddie. I was only ten days into my hospital stay, but when I heard salsa and bachata music—my favorite—I could not resist. I danced with Maddie, holding my stomach, despite the pain. My daughter was worried, telling me not to overdo it, but at that moment, all I cared about was enjoying my time with my granddaughter. I did not think about the pain that would come later; I just lived in that moment, surrounded by my family.

The support from my family, especially my husband, gave me the strength to keep going. I remember hearing about another patient, a police officer, who had been in the hospital for months with burns on just one leg. He did not want to leave the hospital, and there were many patients who were homeless, with no place to go or family to support them. That made me realize how much my family needed me, especially my husband. He told me that he could not live without me and that he wanted to go before me because he would not know what to do if I were gone.

Chapter 17: Pain, Patience, and Perseverance

Even with all the pain and suffering, I found comfort in my faith. When everyone left, and I was alone, I held onto my rosary. After they cleaned my burns, the worst pain came from the nerves. Without pain relief, the agony was unbearable, even worse than the cleaning itself. Managing my pain became the most important part of my hospital stay. I needed morphine every three hours and other medications every five hours. If I missed a dose, I would be in hell again.

CHAPTER 18
ENDURING THE AGONY

After I was moved out of the ICU, things did not really change much for me. The only difference was that I was no longer considered to be in immediate danger. Once I was out, they put me in a regular room. The room was private, so I was by myself. Even though it was a regular room, it was still part of the trauma unit. Being in December, I was surrounded by constant reminders of the holiday season. Christmas was around the corner—festive decorations everywhere. Despite being the worst burn patient in the unit, with 41% of my body burned. I tried to maintain a positive attitude. My family brought a small Christmas tree with lights to my room.

There were other patients there, too, like the policeman who had been there for months with burns on just one leg. Some people had been in car accidents and had been there for a month. In comparison, I had only been there for about eight days when they moved me to the private room.

As soon as I was in the private room, they intensified my physical therapy. A therapist would come to my room every day to help me exercise my legs and hands—most of the early exercises revolved around stretching. They told me that if I did not stretch my skin could contract,

Chapter 18: Enduring the Agony

and I would not be able to move normally again. I did not want that, so I made sure to be ready for my therapy every day. They would arrive around nine o'clock. Before the therapist arrived, I would already be out of bed and sitting in a chair, waiting for them. I managed to do this even though I still had an IV hooked up to me.

The doctors told me that I needed to take in 3,500 calories every day to help my body recover. They encouraged me to eat ice cream and other high-calorie foods. Even with this, they still had the feeding tube in my stomach, providing me with a special protein mixture. It was a high-calorie mixture of protein, minerals, vitamins, and other things. I am not sure exactly what kind of protein they were giving me, but they were very serious about making sure I got those 3,500 calories every day.

A feeding tube is a long and thin tube inserted through the nose and down into the stomach. The nurses kept telling me to swallow until the tube was all the way down to my stomach. They then taped it to my nose to keep it from moving. Then, they would use the tube to put the nutritional mixture directly into my stomach. I remember being on that supplement for about three or four weeks.

Every day, the medical staff kept a close eye on me, constantly checking my wounds. I remember that even after I was moved to a regular room, my bed was always soaked. It was like someone had taken a hose and drenched it. This happened because without skin covering my body,

Chapter 18: Enduring the Agony

fluid would ooze from my wounds. I was wrapped in bandages, and those would get soaked and sticky. The dressing would adhere to my burned areas and were very painful to remove.

Around 11:30 or noon every morning, depending on when the nurses were available, they would come in to scrub me. They could not leave the wet bandages on me because of the risk of infection. So, every morning, during the doctors' rounds at about 6:30 or 7:00, they would let me know when they planned to do my dressing change that day. They would start preparing me about an hour before the dressing change. They would ask if I was ready, and I would always reply yes, even though I dreaded the thought of it.

Sometimes, the nurses were too busy to come right at noon. I would start to think that maybe they would not come at all, and I had gotten a little relief, thinking my body could finally rest without the painful process of changing the bandages. But it never worked out that way. It was crucial for them to change the bandages every day to remove any bad skin and look for potential infections. So, even if they did not come at noon, they would eventually show up at 1:00 or 2:00 in the afternoon.

If they came too late, the medication they had given me earlier would be wearing off. Despite this, they would not give me more medication, no matter how long I had waited. So, the scrubbing and dressing change

Chapter 18: Enduring the Agony

would start, and this happened every single day, right up to the day I was discharged.

Now that I was out of the ICU, I was allowed to have visitors in my room. They still had strict rules—no flowers or anything like that were allowed in my room—all to limit my risk of becoming infected. I was admitted on December 14th 2022. On December 22nd, I was finally moved out of the ICU. The next few days were a blur, and before I knew it, Christmas was approaching.

Despite how heavy it was on their hearts, my daughter, grandkids, and husband brought Christmas to my hospital room. They brought a small Christmas tree, about nine or ten inches tall. They placed all the Christmas presents under that little tree in my hospital room. We celebrated Christmas Day together. We tried our best not to think about the fact that our Christmas was being spent in a hospital room. We even took pictures together, though I could barely move at the time.

Up to this point, I was trying to hold on despite everything. A friend of mine, Dr. G, visited me with her husband. Another friend, Denise, came to see me several times. On one of those visits, Denise found me alone in my room, crying, overwhelmed by pain and despair. She started praying for me. She told me to focus on the parts of my body that were not hurting—like my feet and my hands. She held my foot and prayed and prayed, and to be honest, it actually helped. I could see the tears in

Chapter 18: Enduring the Agony

her eyes. I knew that she wanted to hug me, but she could not because I was covered in bandages. She could see how close I was to giving up.

It was Christmas, and I was supposed to be enjoying the holidays with my grandkids, who had just come from the Philippines. Instead, I was stuck in a hospital bed, unable to even go to the bathroom without help. Every muscle, every nerve in my body was in pain. It was unimaginably difficult to just to get up from the bed, make my way to the bathroom, and come back to sit in a chair.

Despite my family visiting me every day, I still spent much of my day alone. One day, as I sat in my chair, I took a video. I looked at the clock, and all I could think about was how I wished I could turn back time. If only I could go back, I would not be in the position I now found myself in. As I sat there, I thought, *This is it. I am in the hospital with no clue when I will be able to go home to my husband and grandkids.*

Every decision was up to the doctors, not me. This added to the helplessness that I felt. So, every day, I tried to show them that I was able to care for myself. One day, there was no physical therapist because they were busy, so I decided to exercise by myself. My daughter had not arrived yet; she usually came around nine in the morning. They typically did my scrubbing around noon, so I knew I had time. At nine o'clock, I needed to get moving, so I pushed my IV pole and started walking slowly,

Chapter 18: Enduring the Agony

all by myself. I had been out of the ICU for eight days, but I did not want to let anyone stop me from getting better.

The doctors closely monitored my food intake and the supplement they gave me through the feeding tube. Once they saw that I was eating better, they removed the tube. Having that tube was so uncomfortable, and it was such a relief after it was removed. They said I needed to consume 3,500 calories a day, so I drank Ensure, maybe three or four times a day. I tried every flavor—banana, vanilla, and chocolate—until I could not stand it anymore and felt like I wanted to vomit. But I knew I had to keep putting it in my body. The hospital food would arrive, and I would just look at it, having no energy to eat.

My husband visited me every day after work. He would arrive around six or seven in the evening, exhausted but still determined to stay with me for three to four hours before heading home. Our house was an hour and a half away from the hospital, but he did this every single day for five weeks.

For 12 years, I had picked out my husband's work clothes for the day. When his alarm went off at 6:30, I was up too, preparing his breakfast while he showered. His breakfast was simple—bagel with cream cheese, oatmeal with fruit, or toasted bread with butter. I would lay out his clothes, from his shirt and pants to his shoes and belt, even his socks. The only thing I did not pick out for him was his underwear. I figured he could

Chapter 18: Enduring the Agony

manage that on his own. I had done this every day for 12 years, never missing a day.

When I was in the hospital for those five weeks, I continued to help using video chat. Each morning, I would help him pick his outfit. The funny thing is I do not remember any of this. I only know about it now because my family told me about it, and we just laughed about it.

My medication was all about pain management. If they ever forgot to give me my pain meds, I would feel every bit of pain from the procedures they did on me. I needed pain relievers every two or three hours. Even with them, it felt like someone was scraping my skin off. Imagine scrapping your skin off and then how sore it would be afterward. Now, imagine that pain over 41% of your body, more if you include second-degree burns. Every day, the nurses would change shifts—one nurse in the morning and another at night. This is just my experience, but the morning nurses seem different from the night nurses. The morning nurses tended to be more compassionate, giving me all the attention I needed. They never missed my medication, so I felt better during the day. But as soon as the nurses changed, I told my daughter, "Please do not leave until we see who the night nurse is."

There was one incident I still can not fully understand. My husband says I was hallucinating, but I do not think so. It might have been during my third or fourth week in the hospital. A nurse I had never seen before

Chapter 18: Enduring the Agony

came into my room. He was a big guy. He had my morphine and other medications on a tray, but he did not give them to me. Instead, he just walked around my bed, checking my blood pressure and whatever else was on the monitor. It was already two in the morning, and he had missed my scheduled dose. I was in so much pain that I begged him, "Please, I need my medication. I need my morphine." He just replied, "No, I need to check this first," as if my pain did not matter.

I was crying and ended up calling my husband at 2:30 in the morning, waking him up. I told him what was happening, that the nurse had my medication but would not give it to me. My husband asked to speak to the nurse, but the nurse refused. I was in so much pain and could not even find the call button to get help. It seemed to me the nurse had hidden it. My husband told me to scream for help, so I started yelling, "Help! Help!" in the middle of the night, but no one came. I spent the whole night in agony, unable to even get up to go to the bathroom. I was in complete misery.

Finally, around five or six in the morning, they changed shifts. The new nurse came in and cheerfully said, "Good morning, Mrs. Warren." I just stared at him and started crying. He was a young, kind nurse, and he asked, "What happened, Mrs. Warren?" I told him I could not move because I was in so much pain. He was surprised and asked, "Why are you in so much pain? You should have had your medication." I told him I had not received any meds the entire night. When they checked, they

Chapter 18: Enduring the Agony

could not even find the name of the nurse from that night, and I never saw him again. My husband thinks I might have been hallucinating, but I am not so sure. Maybe my brain was playing tricks on me, but my body was definitely feeling the pain.

Every day, I had a routine with the nurses. There were three nurses in my section. The first one, Anthony, was one of the best nurses I had. He was part of the team responsible for scrubbing and dressing my wounds. Anthony was a sweet, young guy, probably 20, 21, or 22 years old, and I think he was either Cuban or Colombian. He would come to me every day and say, "Mrs. Warren, I will be on your team today. I will make sure you are comfortable during your dressing." He was so kind and really cared about me and my comfort.

Another nurse was Shamima. She was from Bangladesh and was about 25 or 27 years old. She treated me like I was her mother. My room became a sort of hangout spot for them. One day, Anthony came in, clearly upset. I asked him what happened, and he told me about a patient who farted in his face while he was cleaning him. He was so mad, and I tried to comfort him. Anthony was a sweet young man, and we often talked about things that were bothering him.

Shamima would also share her stories with me, especially about her family. These nurses really connected with me, and they looked forward to seeing me and I looked forward to seeing them. They wanted to take

Chapter 18: Enduring the Agony

care of me as if I were their family. When they came in the morning, they would often find that I had already taken care of myself as much as I could. I would even change my own gown and bedsheet. I would also clean up as best as I could, even brushing my teeth. I could not brush my hair yet, but I was trying to be as independent as possible.

The nurses would always tell me how happy my room felt. Despite being the sickest patient in the unit, they said my room had the most joyful and positive atmosphere. It made me feel like I did not want to be someone who needed help all the time. I tried to keep things upbeat for everyone around me. I always believed it is better to give and serve others rather than being served. I did not want to be the person who constantly needed help.

Every day, my husband never failed to come to see me. When he came on a Friday night and was not on call the next day, I would ask him to stay with me overnight. He would sleep next to me by the bed, in a recliner chair, and we would hold hands the whole night. I can not put into words the kind of love we have for each other. I never realized just how deeply my husband loves me until this experience. He never left my side.

Whenever he was with me at the hospital, he took care of everything, making sure my medication and rosary were always on my bedside table. Normally, I loved to watch TV, but during this time, I was not interested

Chapter 18: Enduring the Agony

in what was happening in the world. I just wanted to get well and leave the hospital. Music became my mental salve. Every night, I prayed to God, asking to help me through another day.

I had only been in the hospital for a short time when the doctor told my husband I could be there for up to three months. I could not imagine staying that long. I felt like I might die in the hospital.

My husband explained that they could not release me because my surgery and skin grafts were still fresh. The doctors used special bandages with cream inside to help my skin grow faster. These bandages were sterile and had to be carefully placed every day. They placed them over my legs up to my chest.

The worst damage was on my stomach, from below my chest, across from right to left, up to just above my belly button. That entire area needed to be grafted. The skin for the grafts was taken from my back, from my shoulders down to my lower back. This was the only available donor site, and they worried there would not be enough skin to cover everything that needed to be grafted. By the time they did the skin grafting, I was no longer in the ICU. The doctor had waited to allow some healing to occur so they could tell where the grafts were needed the most.

When I came out of the OR (Operating Room), I was under observation for six hours. The doctors were closely watching to see how my body would react to the new skin graft. The first night, I had to sleep

Chapter 18: Enduring the Agony

sitting up because my back was so raw and had no skin left. It was not like the burns on my legs, the skin on my back would grow back relatively quickly. But honestly, my back never returned to normal. To this day, you can see where they harvested the skin for my grafts.

If you look at my back now, you can tell it is not normal skin. It looks like there is a pattern on it. Long strips from my shoulder to my butt. The graft had hatched pattern like a tennis net. They did this so they could stretch the skin to cover my burns. Even now, my skin still feels tight, especially around my stomach. It is been almost two years since the surgery. I realized my body will never be the same again. I can not run or jump like I used to, but I can still play pickleball, which I greatly enjoy.

After leaving the ICU, I was moved to a regular room, but we had no idea when I would be able to go home. I spent Christmas in the hospital, just waiting. The doctors did not want to discharge me until my burns were fully dry because I was at high risk for infection. Fortunately, I did not have any major complications, such as infection or bleeding. The doctors were focused mainly on making sure my road to recovery was as smooth as possible.

CHAPTER 19
STRENGTH IN THE SEASON OF HEALING

I spent Christmas in the hospital. My grandkids, my husband, and my daughter all came to celebrate. They brought a small Christmas tree, and we decorated the room together. On Christmas Day, they brought some food, and we opened presents right there in my hospital. In our family, we have a tradition of giving nine small presents and one big present, so usually our tree is overflowing with gifts. But this year, because it was the hospital, we only brought the biggest present. Even though I could not move much and was stuck sitting, I watched my grandkids open their gifts, and my husband and I exchanged ours, too. We even took some pictures. A few friends came to visit during Christmas, but after they left and the day came to an end, and my husband had to go back to work. There, I was alone again in my hospital bed Christmas night.

After Christmas, on December 26, things were the same. I was slowly recovering, feeling a bit stronger each day. My walking improved, and I no longer needed an IV. When I unplugged the monitor, the nurses knew I was either walking around or in the bathroom. My days were repetitive, but I could feel myself getting better and stronger. The daily medication and dressing changes for my burns continued. It was still

Chapter 19: Strength in the Season of Healing

tiring, though. Every day, around nine o'clock, they would ask when I wanted my dressing change, which took three hours and still required six nurses. By the end, I was always exhausted.

To lift my spirits, I asked my daughter and grandkids to take down the Christmas decorations and put up some for New Year's. Even though I was still in the hospital, I wanted to feel like I was celebrating the holidays.

Before my burns, my husband and I had big plans for New Year's Eve. We had booked a cruise for New Year's Eve, and even a cruise for our wedding anniversary on February 14, 2023. Everything was paid off, but all of it had to be canceled because of my condition.

On New Year's Eve, we watched the countdown in New York on TV. The kids did not come this time; they stayed at home. My husband stayed with me for New Year's Eve as he was not working that night. On New Year's Day, it was a holiday, but I found myself feeling more tired and anxious. Even though I was getting better physically, the loneliness and sadness were overwhelming. I felt like, instead of improving, I was becoming more emotional, especially as I lay there, struggling with how the days seemed to blend into nights.

It was always the same—waking up and trying to shift my focus away from my emotions. I would tell myself that my mind is stronger than my feelings. I would try to think differently and put myself from

Chapter 19: Strength in the Season of Healing

sinking into despair. I was not ignoring my feelings, I was just trying to tell myself there was nothing to worry about.

To distract myself, I would walk down the hallway every day. My walking had improved a lot since I had been exercising my legs regularly. I was not running, but I could walk well enough. I greeted everyone I passed, wishing them Happy New Year or Merry Christmas, just to feel a connection with people. Then I would go back to my room, where they brought food I did not want to eat. I usually just drank Ensure. That became my main food—vanilla, chocolate, whatever flavor they had. To add a little variety to my days, I had my daughter buy Ensure at the store just to get new flavors.

When January came, they examined my burns and my graft. They told me everything was healing well. They looked at the skin grafts on my legs, and though the worst part of my burn was on my stomach, they said they were healing, too. I was still wearing bandages. It felt like I was wearing a top, but it was not—it was all gauze wrapped around me, from my chest down to my stomach. The nurses did a great job with the dressing. They even wrapped me in a way that felt like a bra, but it was just more gauze. By that point, the bandages on my legs were not as extensive, but my stomach still required special care because the skin grafts were not fully healed. It was still wet, so the doctors were cautious, checking it constantly to make sure it was not damaged.

Chapter 19: Strength in the Season of Healing

By late January 2023, I had been in the hospital for five weeks, and I was feeling incredibly bored and sad. I missed my home and did not want to be there anymore. My husband spent the night with me and on the morning of Sunday, January 29, I was laying in bed, feeling an emotional breakdown coming on. I was feeling sorry for myself, and my husband tried to comfort me, telling me how strong I was.

At around seven in the morning, I looked at him and said, "Babe, you need to tell the doctor that I need to go home. If they do not let me go, I am going to escape." After much pleading, I made him promise to take me home. I cried because I did not want him to leave for work the next day while I was still stuck there. I could not stay another day in the hospital.

The night before, I had been praying and praying, asking God to let the doctor send me home. That is all I could do—pray and talk to God. The next morning, around 7 or 7:30, the doctor came in. Before we could say anything, he smiled and said, "Guess what? I have got good news. I think you are going home today."

When the doctor said I could go home, my husband started crying before I did. We hugged each other, even though it was just a small, gentle hug. I told him, "I am going home, babe," and we were both so emotional. The nurses were shocked but happy, too. It was bittersweet for them

Chapter 19: Strength in the Season of Healing

because I had become popular in the unit. They would often come to my room, and now Mrs. Warren was leaving. I could not wait to go home.

My daughter was not there at the time, but my husband and Anthony, my favorite nurse, were there with me. Before I could leave, I needed one last dressing change. They told me that after the dressing, I could go home. By 11 a.m., they were preparing everything—giving me my medication and making sure I was ready to leave. It was not the usual six nurses anymore, just three this time, and by the last day, it had been reduced to two: Anthony and another nurse whose name I can not remember. My burns had been healing, and grafted skin was drying and sticking to the muscle, so they did not need as many nurses to help me.

During the dressing, they talked to my husband and showed him how important it was not to skip any of the care once we got home. They explained that he had to do the dressing every single day, just like they did in the hospital. They even made a video of the whole process, showing how to remove the bandage slowly and carefully. They gave us everything we needed: bandages, cream, medication. They also said I would need to see the doctor in two weeks to check that everything was healing properly.

Finally, it was time to leave. Anthony gave me a little bear with a bandage on its leg and chest. He said, "This is you, a little cute bear." I still have that bear. We took the bandages off it when I no longer needed

Chapter 19: Strength in the Season of Healing

mine. My granddaughter Maddie, who was three at the time, loved the bear.

They took me in a wheelchair to the reception area of the unit. There was a big bell which I did not know what it was for. They told me that when a patient goes home, they get to ring the bell. So, I rang it as loudly as I could, crying at the same time because I was finally going home. They took a picture of me with all the nurses who had helped me.

When it was time to leave the hospital, Anthony helped my husband push the wheelchair. They did not want me to walk too far. Then came the scariest part for me—waiting for the car.

When my husband pulled up, it was the same car he had used to take me to the emergency room. I was hit with a wave of nausea. It brought back memories of that day, the long 45-minute ride to the hospital. My husband kept apologizing, saying, "I am so sorry," but he did not understand what was going on in my mind. My car is bigger, an SUV, and easier for me to get into, but this was the car we used in that difficult moment. Even though it was hard, I held my husband's hand, and we were both happy to finally be heading home.

At home, we have a small workout room, this is where I had done my yoga on that fateful day. Next to it is a powder room, and there is also a small steam room. We converted the gym area into a room for my dressing changes. We set up a massage table where I would lie down, and

Chapter 19: Strength in the Season of Healing

we kept all the medication, bandages, and supplies there. It became a place for my daily care.

My daughter was the one who helped me with the dressing. She is not a nurse or caregiver, but she watched the video the hospital made and learned how to take care of my wounds. She did an amazing job.

The hospital had arranged for a home health nurse to come and help a few days after I got home. When she arrived, she was not sure what to do, and I was still in a lot of pain when the bandages were removed or replaced.

My daughter knew exactly how much pressure to use, but the nurse did not. After one visit, she told me she was not coming back because she had family issues and would be absent for two weeks. I decided then to call the company and tell them not to send any more nurses. My daughter would be my nurse, doing my daily dressing change.

Every morning, Mickie would arrive around 9 a.m., even though she had three kids to take care of—two in high school, one in middle school, and Maddie, who was only three. She would bring Maddie with her and take care of everything, from cleaning me up to washing my hair. She stayed until about 2 or 3 p.m. every day. She did this for two months until I no longer needed the bandages on my legs.

Chapter 19: Strength in the Season of Healing

I remember the first time we removed them all, including the bandages around my waist—it felt like I was wrapped like a mummy before. For every bandage I did not need, a prayer was answered. Finally, I was starting to feel like myself again.

After several weeks of home dressing changes, my daughter looked at my legs and said, "Mom, I do not think we need the bandages anymore. It is dried." I was so proud of myself. I took a picture of my legs and felt really happy, but most of all, I was grateful for my daughter. I could never have done any of this without her. Thinking about it now still makes me emotional.

It is hard to talk about it, and I never really have before. Now that I am off pain relievers and fully awake, I remember everything clearly. The memories are tough. I think about how helpless I felt, unable to move, scared that even the smallest bump could potentially damage my skin. I am still very careful now—nothing is like before. I still get flashbacks, especially when I think about being by the pool. I can picture myself there, crossing my arms and screaming for help. It is not easy, but despite everything, I still love our house. I can not hate it, even with those memories.

One thing I want to add, something important that I forgot to mention earlier—when I first came home from the hospital, everyone was there waiting for me. It was around five or six in the evening, and they had a

Chapter 19: Strength in the Season of Healing

"Welcome Home" sign. My daughter, my grandchildren, everyone was there. And what did I do? Even with my bandages still on, I went into the kitchen and cooked dinner for my family. I was holding my stomach while cooking, everyone was shocked and told me to take it easy, afraid I would hurt myself, but I did not care. I wanted to celebrate my return home, my freedom and my independence.

We have a picture of that moment—everyone chopping and helping out. We were making (Kaldereta) a Filipino dish, beef stew with potatoes and carrots. My husband did not say anything at first, but he was so excited. Then he hugged me, crying, and said, "This house would never be the same without you."

CHAPTER 20
EMBRACING LIFE, ONE TRIP AT A TIME

When the bandages were finally all gone, I was so happy. I felt a glimmer of my old self. The first thing my husband and I did was plan a trip. We had not been able to travel much before the accident, so this was really exciting for us.

Our first trip after the accident was to Sarasota. We are collectors of art, and we had received an invitation to attend an art auction. It was a complimentary stay at the Ritz-Carlton. I thoroughly enjoyed this trip finally feeling free again.

My skin was still sensitive, but the excitement of traveling and feeling independent again was more important to me than the discomfort. This was in May of 2023. It was amazing to think that in January 2023, I had still been in the hospital. I remember coming home on January 29, and Mickie helped me with the dressings until the bandages were completely removed for the last time, sometime in late February.

The first big celebration we had after the accident was for my husband's birthday on February 5, 2023. We also had a housewarming

Chapter 20: Embracing Life, One Trip at a Time

ceremony for the second time, and I called Father Kenny to bless the house again. In the pictures from that day, you can still see me with bandages on my arms, though by then, it was just an arm sleeve with cream underneath.

We invited some friends over and celebrated in a part of the house near where the accident had happened. That day, we also had both of our cars blessed. We had bought them in 2022 before the accident, and in our Filipino culture, it is important to bless new things, like cars. So, Father Kenny did that for us also.

After the housewarming, I continued supporting a foundation that I have been involved with for five years called "The Rose Society." It is part of a nonprofit called "Kids Beating Cancer," which raises money to help defer the expenses associated with cancer treatment for children. I worked with this organization even before my accident. They would plan events, up to a year in advance.

The next big event they had was planned before my accident. It was a huge fashion show at the Four Seasons Hotel by Disney World. This was on April 13, 2023, and it was the second event I attended after the accident. I had a sponsored VIP table and invited friends to attend with me. It was the first big event I attended with my burn scars visible. My skin was still fresh from healing. Despite everything, I tried to act like

Chapter 20: Embracing Life, One Trip at a Time

nothing had happened. On the day after April 14, I was with Kids Beating Cancer again for another event.

Then, on April 26, we took the family and stayed at Disney Animal Kingdom Resort for the weekend. We had a three-bedroom suite and enjoyed our time there, arriving on Friday and checking out on Sunday. It was a wonderful experience, which allowed me to feel like I was becoming somewhat normal again.

In May, I attended another Kids Beating Cancer event called the Royalty Celebration. It was also held at the Four Seasons Hotel. I wore a dress, and everyone thought I looked as if nothing had ever happened. What people could not see was both the scarring and, more importantly, my psychological scar. That was on May 12, 2023.

Our first road trip after the accident was to Sarasota, Florida. That was from May 18 to May 23. In the photos, you can see the scars on my arms. I was still wearing compression sleeves on my legs and a compression bodysuit for my stomach. We stayed at the Ritz-Carlton Hotel and attended an art auction, where we saw many beautiful paintings.

At the restaurant in the hotel, a waitress came to our table and said that I looked so happy. I smiled and said, "Yes, I am." My husband told her, "You would not believe what she is been through. She was burned over 41% of her body just last year." The waitress was surprised, and my

Chapter 20: Embracing Life, One Trip at a Time

husband continued, "Yet here she is, smiling and happy." And it is true, I had no complaints. In every picture, I am smiling because I was—and still am—just happy to be alive.

The following month, in June, we went on another staycation with the grandkids. My daughter and grandkids had just arrived in the US in September 2022, shortly before my accident. They had experienced big culture shock because they had spent their entire childhood in the Philippines. They had attended Montessori school back home, so moving to the US was a huge change for them. My granddaughter, 16, and my grandson, 17, started high school in the public school system. They had to adjust to a completely different culture, and with everything going on after my accident, we did not even realize how much they were dealing with.

Since it was their summer vacation and they had not started school yet, we decided to take them to a Disney hotel, the Saratoga Springs Resort. We stayed there from June 2 to June 9, 2023, enjoying our time together. The kids loved it, and it was a nice break for everyone.

Then, in July, my husband and I went to Las Vegas. That was on July 7, 2023. After surviving the accident, I felt so alive, and I wanted to enjoy every moment I had. I told my husband, "We are not waiting until you turn 70 to retire. You have to retire now so we can enjoy life together."

Chapter 20: Embracing Life, One Trip at a Time

Of course, it did not happen that way, but that trip to Las Vegas was important for us.

In August, we celebrated another special event. On August 18, it was my dear friend DJ Tara's 60th birthday. She was not planning anything big for her milestone birthday, so I invited her to our house. That was the first party I had hosted at the house since my accident, and it was a special moment for me.

That small party we had for DJ Tara's 60th birthday on August 18, 2023, was special. She invited about 15 people to celebrate, and it felt good to host something again, even if it was small. But despite all the positive things happening around me—like the parties, trips, and time with family—I was still struggling with my PTSD and anxiety.

To this day, I can not sleep without taking my nightmare and sleeping pills. I did not even know there were specific pills for nightmares until I started taking them. If I miss even one dose, the nightmares come back, and my husband has to wake me up. This has been my reality every night since the accident.

I did not start seeing a psychologist until almost one and a half years after the accident. This December 14, 2024, will mark my two-year anniversary. But instead of calling it an anniversary, I see it as a celebration of my life, because I survived.

Chapter 20: Embracing Life, One Trip at a Time

One of the best things that happened last year was getting my dog, Shadow. My husband and I used to have two dogs. They were his before we met, a Siberian husky named Kody and a Labrador named Archie. They were more his dogs than mine, but I had known them for a long time. Unfortunately, Archie passed away in 2017, and Kody followed in 2018 because he could not live without Archie. After Kody passed, my husband told me he did not want any more dogs because it was too painful for him, especially since he was always the one who had to take them to be put to sleep.

So, from 2018 onward, we decided not to have any more dogs. But after my accident, one day, I was sitting in my recliner, crying. I felt so alone. Despite all the trips and parties, the sadness and loneliness never left. Every day, I would look at myself in the mirror and see all the scars—my beautiful skin was gone and I was left with scars from my chest to my legs. Even though I kept thanking God for keeping me alive and reminding myself how grateful I was, as a human, those feelings of loneliness and anxiety would still hit me hard. Every time I looked at the lanai and the pool, the flashbacks would come, and I would be overwhelmed with emotions again.

So, one day, I told my husband, "I think I need a dog." He looked at me, and I could tell he could not say no. He simply said, "I think we need a dog now." After that, I started looking online for adoption options. We found a dog rescue and arranged an appointment. The person who ran the

Chapter 20: Embracing Life, One Trip at a Time

dog rescue was Mel. She lived in Ocala, about an hour and a half away from us. She told us she had several dogs available. I was hoping to adopt a husky because I have always loved them, but my husband was a bit hesitant. He was worried because huskies are not always great with small children, and at the time, we had a four-year-old around the house.

Despite the concern, we decided to visit Mel's place. It was a large property with lots of animals—horses, dogs, cats, you name it. Mel's daughter, Cathy, was eight years old at the time, and she was very active and talkative. While we were discussing my accident and why I wanted a dog, Cathy overheard us and said, "Mom, I think Shadow would be the best dog for her."

Mel explained that Shadow was supposed to be Cathy's service dog. However, Shadow did not pass her final test because she got nervous around crowds and would pee. Obviously, this is not acceptable when out in public. So even though Shadow did not pass as a service dog, she had been well-trained. They introduced us to Shadow, and I noticed she had small scars on the tip of both ears. These were the result of fly bites and they looked sore and inflamed. Cathy showed us how Shadow had been trained to wake her up when she had trouble breathing. She was trained to lick her face instead of barking to make sure Cathy woke up. She also showed how she would escort her across the street. Looking both ways before walking. We could tell Cathy was very attached but also knew that

Chapter 20: Embracing Life, One Trip at a Time

she could not keep Shadow any longer. The fact that she thought that Shadow was for us was really special.

Shadow was very smart and well-trained, but when I first met her, there was no connection between us. She did not even look at me. She was clearly attached to Cathy and she was trained to care for her. Still, Mel's family believed Shadow was the right dog for me, so we decided to take her home.

Shadow was a bit strange at first. She is afraid of men and would not come near my husband at all. In fact, it took nearly a year before she got comfortable with him. On the drive home, it was like we had a newborn baby. We went to the pet store to get everything Shadow might need and many things she did not. Looking back, we laugh at all the stuff we bought.

We were so excited when we got Shadow. We bought her a kennel, food, a bed and toys—everything she could need. I was thrilled, Shadow has truly lived up to her name. She has become like my shadow, following me everywhere. Even if she is asleep, if I get up to do something, she will wake up and follow me. It is adorable. Shadow has been one of the best therapies for me. She loves me so much, and she is my constant companion. Every time I come home, she is there to greet me, even though she is not allowed to jump on me, for fear of scratching my damaged skin.

Chapter 20: Embracing Life, One Trip at a Time

After we got Shadow, more events started happening in 2023. In October, we attended the Hats and Heroes Ball, a huge event with about 300 to 400 people to raise money for Kids Beating Cancer. My husband wore a tuxedo, and I wore a gown for the first time. I went without a scarf or jacket to cover my scars. It was a big moment for me, letting my scars show.

We stayed at the Waldorf Hotel for the event. Even now, as I look back, it feels like I am living as if nothing ever happened to me. After that, on October 17, I traveled to Vancouver with my friend Lisa. She was the one who held my hand in the hospital and when I first walked again after the accident. We had planned this trip with a group of friends before everything happened.

While in Vancouver, we went to the Capilano Suspension Bridge. It is a very high, narrow, wood suspension bridge made of wood and rope. The catch is that once you cross the bridge, there is no other way out—you have to come back the same way. People were shaking the bridge as they crossed. I had never liked heights or rollercoasters before, but after what I had been through, I told Lisa that this bridge did not scare me anymore. She even took a video of me crossing it.

Thanksgiving came, and my stepson, Chris, came to visit. In September, we attended another art auction in Key Largo. All of this

Chapter 20: Embracing Life, One Trip at a Time

happened within a year after I came out of the hospital. It feels like life just kept pushing me forward, no matter what.

In December, my husband and I attended a party hosted by Advent Hospital, where he works. It is one of the biggest hospitals in the Orlando area. The theme was sports, so I wore a Dallas Cowboys jersey, and my husband dressed up in a Colorado Avalanche jersey. That was on December 3, 2023.

Then, on December 23, I organized a big Christmas party at our house. Everyone knew about my accident, and my neighbors were shocked when they saw me planning the event. They asked, "Imee, you have been out of the hospital for less than a year. Are you sure you are up for this?" I told them, "The show must go on!" The house was lit up, and I even rented a 360-degree photo booth. Everyone came not just for the party but also to see me for the first time since the accident. It was a night to remember.

On New Year's Eve, we went out for another party. Ever since my accident, my social life has not slowed down. People started calling me a "social butterfly" because of all the events we were attending.

In 2024, we celebrated New Year's Eve at a gala. After that, we made plans to visit the Philippines from January 31 to February 23. It was a special trip because we were celebrating our 10th wedding anniversary. We had originally gotten married in our house in 2014, but after the

Chapter 20: Embracing Life, One Trip at a Time

accident, I told my husband I did not want a fancy vow renewal with a gown. Instead, we celebrated with my family in the Philippines. My kids and grandkids stayed in the US, but my son Nico, his family, and my brothers were all there.

We had a great party planned by a party organizer. Everyone in the Philippines knew about my accident, and as people looked at me, I shared my message: no matter what happens in life—whether it is tragedy or blessing—it is important to be grateful for what we have.

Then one day, while sitting at dinner, the idea of writing a book came up again. People had often told me, "Why do not you write a book and tell your story?" I had brushed it off at first, but during that dinner, I turned to my husband and said, "I think I want to write a book." He fully supported me, and that is how *"Fire and Faith"* was born.

To this date, I look back on my life. All of the good happy times and also, all of the difficult times, too. Each event, large or small, has come to shape the person I have become. These experiences have taught me that no matter what life throws at you, it is only a moment in time and will eventually pass. I have learned to never give up or lose hope. I hope my story inspired you and, in some small way, helps you deal with life's ups and downs.

As a burn survivor, I have come to appreciate the beauty of life in ways I never imagined. Each day is a gift and I feel incredibly grateful to

Chapter 20: Embracing Life, One Trip at a Time

be here, sharing my journey. I understand the challenges that come with surviving trauma. Those days when scars feel heavy, both physically and emotionally, but I want to remind everyone that healing is a journey, not a destination. It is okay to feel overwhelmed, it is part of being human. Through my experiences, I have learned the importance of resilience, self-love and community. I strive to inspire others who are navigating their own path, showing them it is possible to find joy and purpose again. Together, we can help one another, share our stories and remind ourselves that we are not defined by our scars but by our courage to keep moving forward. Let's celebrate our victories, no matter how small and continue to support each other on this incredible journey of healing.

Printed in Great Britain
by Amazon